BOX OFFICE
BIBLE
STUDIES
VOLUME 2

50 Discussion Lessons for Adults

Jim Eichenberger

STANDARD
PUBLISHING

TM

Cincinnati, Ohio

To a cast of characters zanier
than any described in this book—my in-laws:
Nita Hargrave, David Hargrave, Kay (C. L.) Grimes,
Dan Hargrave, and Doug Hargrave.
Thank you for your encouragement, wisdom,
and willingness to critique
and field-test my madness.

Standard Publishing, Cincinnati, Ohio.
A division of Standex International Corporation.

© 2001 by Jim Eichenberger. All rights reserved.
Printed in the U.S.A.
Solid Foundation® is a registered trademark of Standard Publishing.

07 06 05 04 03 02 01   9 8 7 6 5 4 3 2 1

ISBN 0-7847-1286-7
Scripture quotations are taken from the HOLY BIBLE, NEW INTERNATIONAL VERSION®. NIV®.
Copyright © 1973, 1978, 1984 by International Bible Society. Used by permission of
Zondervan Publishing House. All rights reserved.
Edited by Theresa Hayes
Cover design by Liz Howe Design & Illustration
Inside design by Dina Sorn

CONTENTS

Music in Funny Places

USING BOX OFFICE BIBLE STUDIES

Box Office Bible Studies are ideal for home groups, Sunday school, or large group studies. We recommend using them in three ways:

1. Embellish your lessons/sermons/devotions. You have a Bible presentation planned but need an introduction. Use the topical and Scripture indexes on pages 108-112 to locate a usable clip.

2. Try a change of pace lesson. You have just completed a lesson series and want to give the class a one- or two-week "breather" before beginning another. Or you have been called to substitute teach in a class on short notice. Simply find a lesson or two in the table of contents that appeals to you for an easy to teach and prepare study.

3. Put together a short lesson series. String together several of the related studies shown here for a full-fledged series. *Box Office Bible Studies Volume 2* has been designed to briefly cover the scope of biblical history. Try these following combinations:

Pre-History—lessons from humankind's earliest days
    Lessons 50, 25, 27, 21, 32, 39
The Patriarchs—the lives of Abraham, Isaac, Jacob, and family
    Lessons 40, 13, 35, 11, 46, 42
The Life of Moses—important events from the book of Exodus
    Lessons 18, 2, 41, 5, 45, 38
Establishing a Nation—Joshua and the judges
    Lessons 26, 10, 37, 6, 31, 9
One Nation Under God—David and Solomon
    Lessons 30, 24, 1, 17, 47, 16
Rebellion and Restoration—the kingdoms of Israel and Judah
    Lessons 29, 30, 49, 16, 23, 11
New Testament Events—highlights from the Gospels and Acts
    Lessons 28, 15, 49, 22, 36, 7, 34
New Testament Teaching—living for Christ
    Lessons 12, 8, 19, 14, 23, 43, 29

FAQs

Q: WHY WOULD ANYONE USE MOVIE CLIPS TO INTRODUCE A BIBLE STUDY?

A: For the same reason that Jesus used contemporary stories to introduce godly principles: they work! One of the peculiarities of the human mind is its partiality to stories over lists of facts. Jesus told relevant stories to his audience of farmers, fishermen, and housewives; we have an audience of media junkies.

Q: DON'T YOU GLORIFY MOVIES BY USING THEM IN THIS WAY?

A: No. The word used in the New Testament that we translate "glory" originally referred to weight. Something was glorified if it was given weight or shown to have value. Movies have already been glorified (whether rightly or wrongly) by our media-hungry culture. Because of this, movies can be used to give weight to God's Word. Jesus met his hearers on common ground. From there he walked with them to higher ground—an understanding of God's nature and purposes. *Box Office Bible Studies* attempt to meet the media culture on common ground and invite them to the higher ground of the Word of God.

Q: SHOULDN'T WE BE STUDYING THE BIBLE RATHER THAN MOVIES?

A: Of course! These lessons are not studies of movies any more than Jesus' parables were studies of farming and fishing! These familiar movie clips will direct our audience to study God's Word but will never seek to overshadow or replace it.

Q: DOESN'T THE USE OF A MOVIE CLIP ENDORSE QUESTIONABLE ACTIONS OF THE CHARACTERS?

A: If we held Jesus' parables to that standard, would we have any left? The protagonists of some of Jesus' stories were more than a little shady. Jesus did not endorse the theological position of the Good Samaritan, the sins of the tax collector, or the business practices of the shrewd manager. Likewise using movies as parables is not intended to endorse the actions of the characters, the actors that portray them, or the companies that produce them.

Q: WHY DO YOU SUGGEST SOME MOVIES THAT CONTAIN OBJECTIONABLE CONTENT?

A: Three steps were taken in choosing clips for *Box Office Bible Studies:* First, the clips come from popular movies. The rational for using movie clips (as stated above) is to grab an audience's attention with familiar content. Clips were chosen from the American Film Institute's (AFI) lists of favorite movies and for their availability in the most popular video rental chains or public libraries.

Second, the clips must be free of objectionable content. No suggested clips contain profanity, sexual situations, nudity, graphic violence, or illegal drug use. The movies from which these clips are taken may include such elements, but the suggested clips do not.

Third, the clips must contain content that will effectively introduce a biblical theme. The films may not always show a positive example of a biblical principle, but bad theology can be used to teach good theology. Jesus' parables often used negative examples to teach positive behavior.

Q: WILL SOME BE OFFENDED BY THIS APPROACH?

A: No one method of teaching or curriculum is for everyone. A church or class needs to choose methods and materials that will reach its intended audience. These books are not for everyone.

Although clips are chosen carefully, the teacher must screen clips to make sure that they are appropriate for his or her class. Every teacher may not want to use every clip in these books. It is better not to use a clip than to offend your audience.

Q: HOW DO COPYRIGHT LAWS APPLY TO THIS USE OF MOVIES?

A: Movies are protected by copyright. If you rent, borrow, or purchase a video, you are agreeing to use it only for private home viewing. Public use, especially when an admission fee is charged, could be a copyright violation. The doctrine of fair use, however, permits certain uses of brief excerpts from copyrighted materials for not-for-profit teaching purposes without written permission. You should check with your church's legal counsel for more complete information regarding your specific situation. For churches that use film clips regularly, we recommend applying for a blanket licensing agreement from the Motion Picture Licensing Corporation at 800-462-8855, or http://www.mplc.com.

Q: HOW DO I FIND THE CLIP ON MY VIDEO?

A: The beginning and ending times given for each clip are taken from the beginning of the movie, not of a specific tape. (Some versions have previews and other advertising.) *Set your counter to zero when the studio credit fades.* Even given the variables of tapes and equipment, you should be within ten seconds of the desired clip. For further help, dialogue and a scene description is included. NOTE: All clips are free of profanity, overt sexual content, and graphic violence. To avoid these objectionable features, you will need to cue your tape accurately.

ARROGANCE OF POWER

2 Samuel 11

TO BEGIN

Before the session, find or sketch large pictures of a knife, a gun, and a stick of dynamite. As the session begins, hold up one picture after another asking, "For what is this used?" Although all of these have uses other than inflicting violence upon another person, what responses were common? Perhaps this visitor from another planet has a point.

THE CLIP

Aliens whose first eight plans for getting humankind's attention didn't work try Plan 9—reanimating corpses.

Though the movie is not a comedy, this explanation by alien Eros (Dudley Manlove) of why mankind must be destroyed is unintentionally hilarious.

FOR DISCUSSION

🎥 According to Eros, why must humankind be destroyed? What is his reasoning? With what points of his argument do you agree? The Bible also talks about how humans misuse power. The story of David is a prime example.

🎥 Close your eyes. Imagine that you have become president of the company for which you work. You are now in your office, leaning back in your overstuffed chair with your feet on the desk. Describe how your position of power makes you feel. How is your state of mind similar to what David's must have been (2 Samuel

11:1)? Note that David had recently come from an impressive string of military victories and had secured the borders of his nation (2 Samuel 8, 10). Paraphrase the words of Hebrews 6:7-12 as a warning to David and others who let their arrogance make them lazy.

⚏ Summarize the teaching of Proverbs 6:20-32. Who wrote those words (Proverbs 1:1)? This passage begins with the warning to "keep your father's commands" and to not "forsake your mother's teaching" (6:20). Who were this writer's parents (2 Samuel 12:24)? How do you feel about these teachings knowing how Solomon's parents met (2 Samuel 11:2-4)? Did David feel that because of his position he could play with fire (Proverbs 6:27, 28) without consequence?

⚏ The powerful often have the arrogance to manipulate others for their own purposes. Read 2 Samuel 11:5-17 and list the ways David tried to manipulate Uriah to rid himself of responsibility. What is the ultimate result when we devalue others (Matthew 5:21, 22)?

⚏ List possessions (house, car, etc.) or positions (manager, father, etc.) that empower you. Describe ways that you could use each arrogantly and use each compassionately.

IN CONCLUSION

David allowed his power to be an excuse to be lazy. He compounded the problem by believing that power gave him license to fulfill his lusts. Finally, his abuse of power led him to attempt control of others, resulting in murder. Stupid . . . stupid . . . stupid.

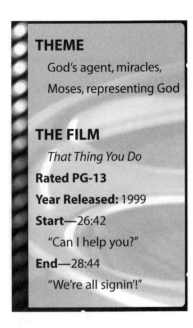

BEING GOD'S AGENT

Exodus 4:1-9

TO BEGIN

Ask each member of the group to list his or her three outstanding characteristics along with his or her name on a note card. Collect the cards. Randomly choose a card and read the characteristics. Can the rest of the group identify the person? Why is what you're doing similar to what the person in this clip wants to do?

THE CLIP

An Erie, Pennsylvania, pop band scores a hit in 1964 and rockets to fame with lots of help from its manager (Tom Hanks).

Agent Phil Horace (Chris Ellis) approaches the band with a proposition to represent them.

FOR DISCUSSION

☞ What does an agent do? What did Phil hope to accomplish as he represented the Oneders? Although we rarely use the term, God's people throughout history have acted as God's agents. They sought to tell others of God's characteristics in order to make his name known. In the story of Moses we learn what is required of God's agent.

☞ A shepherd's staff was simply a large stick that the shepherd found and used as a tool for his profession. It cost nothing and he did nothing to shape it or make it valuable. With that in mind, what did the first miracle God gave Moses say about God's power (Exodus 4:1-5)? Would the miracle have said less about God if it were done with a valuable gold-trimmed, pearl-handled walking stick that Moses had skillfully hand-crafted? Refer to 1 Corinthians 1:26-31 to explain.

☞ Describe the second miracle God gave Moses (Exodus 4:6-8). What normally happened to someone who had leprosy (Numbers 5:1-4)? Referring to Psalm 103:1-4 and Ephesians 2:12, 13, summarize the meaning of this second miracle given to Moses.

☞ Why would you guess that the sight of blood makes some people queasy? If a lot of blood is spilled, what is the probable result? Note that the people of Israel were held captive in Egypt. Also understand that the Nile River was worshiped by the people of Egypt as a god who provided for and nourished the people. With all of that in mind, explain the meaning and probable impact of the third miracle given to Moses (Exodus 4:9; Luke 1:68-75).

☞ As the Oneders agent, Phil Horace had the goal of getting their song on the radio. As God's agent, Moses had the goal of freeing Israel from Egypt. You have also been given the job of being God's agent. What specific goal do you seek to accomplish in that capacity this week?

IN CONCLUSION

The miracles God gave Moses to perform as his agent revealed important truths. As God's agent Moses demonstrated that God empowers the ordinary, that God cleanses the hopeless, and that God delivers the weak from the powerful.

OTHER APPLICATIONS
Use this clip to introduce a sermon, lesson, or devotion on representing God from 2 Corinthians 4.

INSIDE INFORMATION
The four actors playing the Oneders rehearsed as a band for eight weeks to get the feel of performing. However, other musicians dubbed most of their performances in the film.

THEME

calling upon God, Elijah
and the prophets of Baal

THE FILM

Dirty Rotten Scoundrels

Rated PG

Year Released: 1988

Start—20:00

"Alright, what am I going
to do?"

End—21:11

"We're like this!"

CALLING UPON GOD
1 Kings 18:16-39

TO BEGIN

Tell about a time that someone came to your aid
when you were desperate for help. Consider this
case of a man needing a friend.

THE CLIP

Con men Lawrence Jamison (Michael Caine) and
Freddy Benson (Steve Martin) swindle wealthy
women in the south of France.

In this scene Freddy tries to recall the name of his
recent acquaintance, Jamison, to help him out of a
scrape with the law.

FOR DISCUSSION

☞ Describe Freddy's situation. How would you
describe his relationship to Jamison at this point? Do
you think he has a chance of getting real help? Why
or why not? The Bible contains a powerful account
of how God answers those who call to him.

☞ Compare Elijah's conversations in 1 Kings 18:16-
24 to Paul's words to the Galatians (6:7-9).
Explain how Paul would apply the principle of
which he speaks to Ahab, to Elijah, to the
prophets of Baal, and to the people of Israel.
Review the events that had already occurred in
Ahab's reign by skimming 1 Kings 16:29-18:15 as
necessary. Note how people tried to avoid
accepting consequences for their choices.

☞ Consider the question, "Why should I accept

Christianity when many people hold beliefs that are quite different just as fervently?" Formulate a response by reading 1 Kings 18:25-29; Psalm 115:3-8; Habakkuk 2:18-20; and Matthew 7:15-23.

📽 Describe the impossible situations spoken of in 1 Kings 18:30-39; Matthew 17:14-20; Luke 1:30-37; and Luke 18:18-27. Summarize what God says about impossibilities.

📽 Think of a problem you now face. Consider the truths of this lesson: When we call out to God for help we must 1) Admit ways that we have contributed to our predicament; 2) Examine the truth of our beliefs regardless of how strongly we hold them; and 3) Trust God though the situation seems hopeless. Plan to travel one of these roads this week.

IN CONCLUSION

The circumstances of our life are often a result of our response to God's truth (1 Kings 18:16-24). The sincerity or fervency of our belief is meaningless if the object of our belief is powerless (vv. 25-29). Yet no situation is hopeless when God has a hand in it (vv. 30-39). His is a name to remember!

OTHER APPLICATIONS

Use this clip to introduce a sermon, lesson, or devotion on calling upon God for help from Nehemiah 1; Psalm 7; or Luke 18:9-14.

"SCENE" HIM BEFORE?

The director of this film, Frank Oz, is arguably one of the least recognized of Hollywood stars. As a puppeteer he gave life to Miss Piggy, Fozzie Bear, Cookie Monster, and other Muppets. He directed hit comedies such as *Bowfinger* (1999), *House Sitter* (1992), *What About Bob?* (1991), and *Little Shop of Horrors* (1986). His face remains unfamiliar despite starring in some of the most popular films of all time—as the voice of Yoda in the Star Wars series!

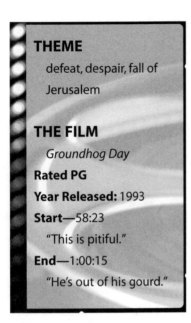

DEFEAT

2 Kings 25:1-12

TO BEGIN

Have you ever been on a sports team? Tell of your team's most humiliating defeat. How did you feel after the game? Were you nearly as depressed as this man?

THE CLIP

Weatherman Phil Conners (Bill Murray) keeps living Groundhog Day over and over again.

Finally, complete despair and desperation overtake Phil.

FOR DISCUSSION

☞ Even though your defeat in sports was humiliating, you still had another game coming in which to redeem yourself. What was Phil's reason for despair? Have you ever hit bottom in your life? At one point in biblical history, God's people bottomed out. Let's examine that event.

☞ Read 2 Kings 25:1-3. In a Bible encyclopedia or dictionary, discover what it meant in the ancient world to be "under siege." From the dates given in this text, calculate the length of time Jerusalem was under siege. Try to describe how you might feel as you awoke in the morning during this time. What would the situation do to your motivation and your energy level? What are some situations people face today that are emotionally similar to being under siege? (A prolonged illness? A difficult marriage?)

👁 Continue reading 2 Kings 25:4-10. Make a list of what was destroyed during the end of this battle. Imagine a resident of Jerusalem at that time saying, "As long as we still have _____, there is hope that _____." Take an item from your list and put it in the first blank. Then complete the sentence. What would be the effect of having each of these destroyed? Do you know of anyone who is at the point of having one final hope? What can you do for that person?

👁 Have you ever said, "At least it can't get worse"? How did this hopeless situation become worse for the people of Jerusalem (2 Kings 25:11, 12)? Have you ever experienced culture shock, being in a strange place without any way of contacting home? How was this situation even worse?

👁 Now that you have seen how bleak life was for those in Judah, think of the toughest problem you face right now. Is there reason for hope?

IN CONCLUSION

The fall of Jerusalem is a picture of ultimate despair. The people of Judah saw no end to their plight. They saw people and places in which they put their hope obliterated. Finally, they experienced severe culture shock, being forced from familiar surroundings. But even that winter would end!

OTHER APPLICATIONS

Use this clip to introduce a sermon, lesson, or devotion on despair from Psalm 137.

OOPS!

The real Gobbler's Knob in Punxsutawney is on the outskirts of town, embedded in a wooded area, not in the center of town.

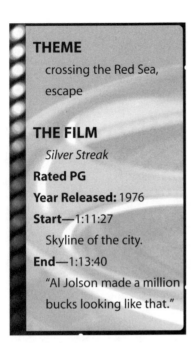

THEME
crossing the Red Sea, escape

THE FILM
Silver Streak
Rated PG
Year Released: 1976
Start—1:11:27
Skyline of the city.
End—1:13:40
"Al Jolson made a million bucks looking like that."

ESCAPE

Exodus 14:13-31

TO BEGIN

Buy a few Chinese finger puzzles at a novelty store. Though most group members will be familiar with them, the devices are still fascinating since the logical means of escape just doesn't work. How logical is this plan of escape?

THE CLIP

Book editor George Caldwell (Gene Wilder) goes on a rail trip from Los Angeles to Chicago. He is caught in a web of intrigue when he thinks that he sees a murdered man thrown from the train.

In this scene, Grover Muldoon (Richard Pryor) schemes to help George escape by disguising him.

FOR DISCUSSION

☞ If someone actually tried such an escape, what might be some of the results? Have you ever tried to get out of trouble with an "it seemed like a good idea at the time" approach? The Bible demonstrates some more reliable principles for escaping from those who would harm us.

☞ The Egyptians did not have to be destroyed. Most scholars agree that the statement, "God hardened their hearts," is best understood to mean that God allowed the Egyptians to follow the direction they had already chosen. What internal attitude and external actions sealed their fates (Exodus 14:15-18)? Consider the advice Gamaliel gave to the Jews who were persecuting the church (Acts 5:38,

39). Why would the Egyptians have been wise to heed that line of reasoning? Is there a place of ultimate security and victory (Matthew 16:18)?

🎬 What is some behavior that could be described as risky? What are the risks of the behavior you describe? Are there dangers in being near someone who is engaged in risky behavior? How can you avoid risk? Think of the risks the Egyptians took in entering the parted sea. How did God protect the Israelites from the same fate (Exodus 14:19, 20)? From that incident and the teaching of Paul (2 Corinthians 6:14-18), describe a good way of escaping destruction.

🎬 Read Exodus 14:21-31. According to Moses, why were the Israelites able to escape harm (Exodus 15:13)? How does this incident illustrate the spiritual truth of Romans 8:12-14 and Galatians 5:16?

🎬 On a piece of paper the size of a business card, write the following escape plan options: Do nothing and wait for your enemy to fail; Get away from those who are heading for trouble; Take decisive action as God directs. Keep the card in your wallet, reviewing your options should trouble arise.

IN CONCLUSION

Like Moses and the Israelites, we can escape when we "stand firm and . . . see the deliverance the Lord will bring" (Exodus 14:13). We escape defeat when our enemies have the vanity to oppose God. We escape destruction when we separate ourselves from those opposing God. We escape into eternal freedom when we follow as our God leads.

OTHER APPLICATIONS

Use this clip to introduce a sermon, lesson, or devotion on escaping the wrath of our enemies from Acts 12:1-19.

OOPS!

As George and Grover arrive in "Kansas City," a long shot of the city clearly shows the Calgary Tower, a unique and unmistakable landmark with no equivalent in Kansas City. The film, of course, was shot in Canada.

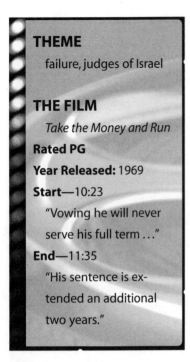

THEME
failure, judges of Israel

THE FILM
Take the Money and Run
Rated PG
Year Released: 1969
Start—10:23
"Vowing he will never
serve his full term ..."
End—11:35
"His sentence is extended an additional
two years."

FAILING HABITUALLY
Judges 2:10-20

TO BEGIN

Tell a story about your life beginning with the words, "It seemed like a good idea at the time." Here is a story that could begin the same way.

THE CLIP

Career criminal Virgil Starkwell (Woody Allen) struggles with life and love in this mock documentary.

In this scene, Virgil tries to escape from prison with a bar of soap carved to look like a gun, but does not count on a change in the weather.

FOR DISCUSSION

☛ What did Virgil do that seemed to give his plan a good chance of succeeding? What unexpected event brought about failure? The Bible tells of a period in the history of Israel in which it seemed nothing went right. Let's discover why.

☛ The book of Deuteronomy recounts the words Moses gave to the people before they entered the Promised Land. In the following verses, circle the command of Moses common to all: Deuteronomy 4:9, 23; 6:12; and 8:11. Compare that command to the behavior of the nation of Israel recorded in Judges 2:10.

☛ Theologians talk about a "God-shaped hole" inside of everyone. What do you think that means? How did the people of Israel fill that hole after they forgot about their God who once filled it (Judges 2:11-15)? The prophet Jeremiah described these actions symbolically (Jeremiah 2:13). Explain how Jeremiah's words apply here.

☞ Peter uses two animal proverbs to describe those who refuse to follow God even though they know better (2 Peter 2:22). What does the word "forfeit" mean? Rewrite those proverbs without using the animal references but using that word instead. Compare your new proverb to the actions you see in Judges 2:16-19.

☞ Find the word "remembrance" (KJV) or a related word in each of these verses: 1 Corinthians 11:24, 25; Philippians 1:3-6; 2 Timothy 1:5; and 2 Peter 3:1, 2. How can these remembrances keep you from falling into a pattern of habitual failure? Are there any of these remembrances that you need to keep more faithfully?

IN CONCLUSION

The history of the judges gives us a foolproof recipe for failure. We will fail when we forget who God is and what he has done for us. We will fail when we forsake the commands God calls us to follow. We will fail when we purposely forfeit the blessings God has for us and stubbornly go our own way.

OTHER APPLICATIONS

Use this clip to introduce a sermon, lesson, or devotion on avoiding failure from Ecclesiastes 12:1-7.

INSIDE INFORMATION

One hundred San Quentin prisoners were paid a small fee to appear in the prison sequences of the film. The cast and crew were stamped each day with a special ink that glowed under ultraviolet light so the guards could tell who was allowed to leave the prison grounds at the end of the day.

THEME

Ananias and Sapphira, lies, pretense

THE FILM

My Man Godfrey

Not Rated

Year Released: 1936

Start—40:14

"These flowers just came for you, Miss."

End—41:51

Laughter

FATAL LIES

Acts 5:1-11

TO BEGIN

As a youngster, did you ever pretend you were ill to avoid going to school? How convincing were you? Here is a clip of an act no one is buying.

THE CLIP

Godfrey Parke (William Powell), a bum living in the city dump, becomes the butler to the family of spoiled heiress Irene Bullock (Carole Lombard).

In this scene, Irene displays an insincere fit of emotion, not fooling anyone, especially the dispassionate Godfrey.

FOR DISCUSSION

☞ What did Irene hope to accomplish with her emotional display? Do you believe her act helped or hindered her cause? What might be some consequences of this snit? The Bible tells us of a couple whose deceptive act had great cost.

☞ Display four or five different cosmetic products for men or women. What does each product do? What does one seek to accomplish by using such products? What spiritual "cosmetic" did Ananias and Sapphira seek to apply (Acts 5:1, 2, 8)? Do you believe their motives were similar to those described in Matthew 23:5-7? Explain. Consider Jesus' words in Matthew 23:13. How might have Ananias and Sapphira's spiritual cosmetics discouraged others from serving God?

⌖ While Ananias and Sapphira attempted to deceive others in the church, to whom were they really lying (Acts 5:3, 4)? In what way or ways is lying the opposite of confessing? Why is lying to God so dangerous? Explain by using the thoughts found in 1 John 1:8–2:2.

⌖ After reading Acts 5:5, 6, 9-11 and John 8:39-47, do you agree that God seems to take lying more seriously than we do? Why is lying an offense worthy of disinheritance in God's eyes?

⌖ Imagine a lie detector aimed at you from Heaven at this very moment. If it were to detect the biggest falsehood in your life right now and display it on a screen for all to read, what would it say? How would such a revelation change your life? Take the following steps this week: Confess this falseness to God daily. Ask God to give you strength to overcome that specific sin. Consider finding a Christian friend to whom you can confess your struggle and to whom you can be accountable.

OTHER APPLICATIONS
Use this clip to introduce a sermon, lesson, or devotion on lying from Proverbs 6:12-19.

OOPS!
As Godfrey arranges flowers in the vase, they keep disappearing and reappearing!

IN CONCLUSION

Ananias and Sapphira lied about their own righteousness, lies offensive to a God of grace and truth. As a result, they paid a terrible price. Remember that we can receive God's incredible mercies only when we are honest with him about who we are. And why not? We certainly aren't fooling him!

THEME

Christian living, first things, priorities

THE FILM

Bring It On

Rated PG-13

Year Released: 2000

Start—31:35

"Ladies and gentlemen, put your hands together for the Rancho Carne Toros!"

End—32:55

"C'mon guys, let's do that cheer."

FIRST THINGS

Matthew 5–7

TO BEGIN

Make two lists. The first list should contain things we do for which the order in which we do them does not matter (e.g., brushing our teeth and washing our face or putting on a shirt and putting on slacks). The second list should contain things we do for which the order does matter (e.g., putting toothpaste on the brush and brushing our teeth, putting on underwear and putting on slacks). Consider the order of events as presented in this clip.

THE CLIP

The cheerleading squad of a southern California high school seeks another national championship.

In this scene, it is obvious that the Rancho Carne cheerleading squad is valued more highly than its pitiful football team. The crowd does not respond with applause until the cheerleaders take the field!

FOR DISCUSSION

☞ What events seem out of order here? What does this order reveal about the priorities of the fans of Rancho Carne High? Can misplaced priorities affect a person's behavior? In his Sermon on the Mount, Jesus talks a lot about "first things."

☞ Read Matthew 5:23, 24. What should be done "first" according to Jesus? Compare these words with Hosea 6:6-9 and Micah 6:6-8. What two aspects of religious practice are discussed in each? Which behavior does God value most, ceremonial actions or kindness to others? Why do you believe that to be true? Do we prioritize these behaviors in the same order as God does? What are some practical ways we can demonstrate "true religion" (James 1:27)?

☞ Read Matthew 6:31-34. What should be done "first" according to Jesus? Compare these words with Ecclesiastes 5:10-15 and 1 Timothy 6:6-10. Is seeking wealth always wrong? Explain. How can "putting first things first" make a difference when it comes to our life's ambitions?

☞ Read Matthew 7:3-5. What should be done first according to Jesus? Consider the account in Luke 7:36-50. How does this story demonstrate the truth of Jesus' "plank and speck" illustration?

☞ By not putting relationship with Jesus first, we can create a religion that is too ritualistic, materialistic, or judgmental. Which of these three adjectives describes your biggest temptation to compromise your faith?

IN CONCLUSION

In his Sermon on the Mount, Jesus told how his disciples would place ministry to people before ceremony, personal godliness before acquisition of property, and self-examination before condemnation of others.

OTHER APPLICATIONS

Use this clip to introduce a sermon, lesson, or devotion about priorities from any of these texts: Matthew 6:33; 19:16-30; Mark 12:28-34; Luke 9:57-62; Revelation 2:1-7.

OOPS!

In order to make a movie that features the leadership of teens, the producers overlook an important fact. A cheer squad cannot compete in this kind of competition without an adult coach/sponsor.

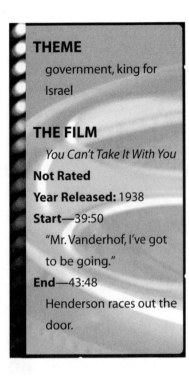

THEME
government, king for Israel

THE FILM
You Can't Take It With You
Not Rated
Year Released: 1938
Start—39:50
"Mr. Vanderhof, I've got to be going."
End—43:48
Henderson races out the door.

FOLLOW THE LEADER
1 Samuel 8:1-22

TO BEGIN
President John Kennedy challenged, "Ask not what your country can do for you, but ask what you can do for your country." What do you think of that advice? What do you believe these characters might say about it?

THE CLIP
A young executive (Jimmy Stewart) falls in love with his secretary (Jean Arthur), a member of a creative, but very eccentric, family.

In this scene, Grandfather Vanderhof (Lionel Barrymore) argues about the value of government with Henderson (Charles Lane), an IRS agent.

FOR DISCUSSION
☞ Summarize the arguments of Vanderhof and Agent Henderson. Who would win the argument? Which argument makes the most sense to you? Explain. Perhaps some of those questions should have been asked when the people of Israel were establishing a government.

☞ In the debates leading up to the 1992 United States presidential election, candidate Bill Clinton promised, that if elected, he would bring about the "most moral administration" in the history of the nation. Do the desires of the elders of Israel in 1 Samuel 8:1-5 remind you of that promise? Explain. How might Jesus respond if asked if human legal authority alone could make people behave morally? His words in Matthew 15:1-11 may help you.

⌨ Agree or disagree: "A strong government will impartially protect the rights of every citizen." How are the words of 1 Samuel 8:6-18 relevant to this question? What besides government is necessary to ensure justice for all (Psalm 9:7-10)?

⌨ Review the events that had already taken place in Israel's history before this incident: Crossing of the Red Sea (Exodus 14); attack on Jericho (Joshua 6); and the victory of Gideon (Judges 7). With those instances in mind, what sounds foolish when you read the words of 1 Samuel 8:19, 20? Explain.

⌨ Copy the words of 1 Peter 2:16, 17 on a note card. Memorize those words this week, asking God to help you understand what government can and cannot do.

IN CONCLUSION

Civil government is ordained by God to keep social order, but we sin when we expect it to do what only God can. Government alone cannot ensure morality, prevent exploitation, or bring security. Those painful lessons were forgotten and taught time and time again throughout the history of Israel.

OTHER APPLICATIONS

Use this clip to introduce a sermon, lesson, or devotion on government from John 19:1-16 or Romans 13.

INSIDE INFORMATION

When this movie was filmed, Barrymore had such severe arthritis that he needed to walk with crutches. To remedy the situation, the director (Frank Capra) fitted him with a cast and explained in the script that his eccentric character injured his foot sliding down a banister.

THEME
Joshua and Jericho, following God's commands

THE FILM
Shanghai Noon
Rated PG-13
Year Released: 2000
Start—21:00
Chon washes his face.
End—24:34
Chon looks up and sees warriors on the hills above him.

FOLLOWING GOD'S PLAN
Joshua 5:13–6:27

TO BEGIN

In a list of "Reasons Why It Is Great to Be a Man," a wit included "Wedding plans just seem to take care of themselves!" Have a (non-violent) member of the opposite sex explain the humor of this statement. Then watch this clip.

THE CLIP

Chon Wang (Jackie Chan) leaves his post as an imperial guard in China to seek a kidnapped princess held captive in the American Old West.

In a scene typical of all Jackie Chan movies, Chon uses every available prop in the landscape in his battle against his enemies.

FOR DISCUSSION

🎬 Does this scene give you the impression that Chon relied more upon a set battle plan or upon his instincts? Explain. In reality, however, do you believe that this fight scene was as unplanned as it seems? In making the film, how much planning probably went into it? Likewise, God's work on earth does not just happen. The story of Joshua tells us that leaders take specific steps in accomplishing God's will.

🎬 Read Joshua 5:13-15. Does the answer given by the angel seem a little unexpected to you? Why? Does it make more sense if one were to paraphrase Joshua's question, "Did you come to join my army or the army of my enemy?" Explain.

How does Joshua's response indicate that he understood that the angel had come to recruit him? Compare this situation to Jesus' words to his disciples in John 15:16.

☛ Describe the battle plan God gave to Joshua (6:1-5). Looking at the plan from a purely military perspective, list as many reasons as you can why it could never work. How do Solomon's words in Proverbs 3:5, 6 seem to apply to Joshua in this situation? Using Solomon's words as an outline, retell the events of the story of Joshua and Jericho.

☛ Many argue today that one's faith is personal and that one has no right to call others to join him or her in it. How might have this story ended if Joshua had felt this way? Read the remainder of this account (6:6-27). What was accomplished with an army that could not have been accomplished by individuals alone? How did Paul describe that principle of leadership in 2 Timothy 2:1-4?

☛ Find a hymnal and review the words of "Onward, Christian Soldiers," "Faith Is the Victory," and "Stand Up, Stand Up for Jesus." As you sing one of them, commit yourself anew to fighting under God's command.

IN CONCLUSION

Joshua did not simply charge wildly into battle. He first placed God's agenda before his own (5:13-15). He accepted God's strategy as his own (6:1-5). Then he led others into God's battle (6:6-27).

OTHER APPLICATIONS

Use this clip to introduce a sermon, lesson, or devotion about waging war God's way from 2 Corinthians 10:1-6; Ephesians 6:10-20; or 2 Timothy 4:6-8.

INSIDE INFORMATION

Although Jackie Chan is a fairly recent box office favorite in this country, he has been making movies since the early 1960s.

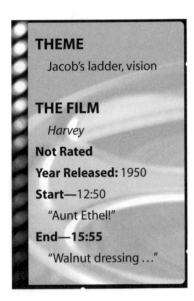

THEME
Jacob's ladder, vision

THE FILM
Harvey
Not Rated
Year Released: 1950
Start—12:50
"Aunt Ethel!"
End—15:55
"Walnut dressing …"

A GLIMPSE OF HEAVEN
Genesis 28:10-22

TO BEGIN

Play "I have never." Give each group member an equal number of beans or other markers. Allow each person to make a statement beginning, "I have never seen/been/owned/eaten, etc." It should be a true statement, but one that the person believes few others could make. For example, one person might say, "I have never eaten cauliflower." Each person who has seen/been/owned/eaten what the speaker has not must give a marker to that speaker. The person with the fewest markers after everyone plays has obviously done the most. Here is someone who has seen something no one else has.

THE CLIP

Elwood P. Dowd (James Stewart) is a mild-mannered, pleasant man, who just happens to have an invisible friend, a six-foot, three and one-half inch rabbit.

In this scene, Elwood embarrasses his family by introducing Harvey to his aunt Ethel (Grayce Mills).

FOR DISCUSSION

☞ What does Elwood see that no one else does? How does that cause others to react to him? Would you want the opportunity to see something that no one else could see? Why or why not? Jacob was a man who had a unique glimpse into God's kingdom. Let's examine what he saw and how he responded.

☞ Describe Jacob's vision in Genesis 28:10-14.

Compare and contrast this structure with the one in Genesis 11:1-9. Notice the builder(s), the size, the purpose, and the will of God concerning each structure. How does this comparison illustrate the truth of Ephesians 2:8, 9? What does Jacob's ladder ultimately represent (John 1:51)?

🎞 What is the significance of the name "Bethel" (Genesis 28:19)? Was it an appropriate name for that place? Read Genesis 28:15-19. In what sense was Jacob's understanding of the "house of God" too limited? Compare these other verses about the presence of God: Joshua 1:5; Matthew 1:23; 28:20; and 1 Corinthians 3:16. Where is the true Bethel?

🎞 What promise does Jacob make after his vision (Genesis 28:20-22)? What is expected of those who have seen the fulfillment of Jacob's vision (Jesus himself)? Read Matthew 19:16-30.

🎞 Write the words of Genesis 28:15 on a note card. Carry it with you and memorize it this week. How might that vision change you?

THE CONCLUSION

The difference between a visionary and a crackpot is the truth of what is seen. A true visionary sees that we are saved by God's grace, not our works. A true visionary finds God's presence everywhere he goes. A true visionary responds to what he sees with a surrendered life. Even Jacob had difficulty comprehending the glimpse of Heaven he was allowed to see.

OTHER APPLICATIONS

Use this clip to introduce a sermon, lesson, or devotion about visions of God's glory from Isaiah 6 or Revelation 1.

INSIDE INFORMATION

At the very end of the movie's credits Harvey opens a door and the words at the bottom of the screen say "Harvey as Himself."

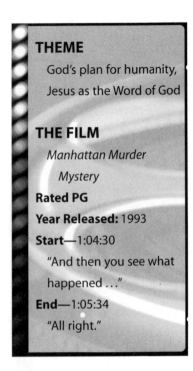

THEME
God's plan for humanity, Jesus as the Word of God

THE FILM
Manhattan Murder Mystery
Rated PG
Year Released: 1993
Start—1:04:30
"And then you see what happened ..."
End—1:05:34
"All right."

GOD'S LAST WORD
Hebrews 1:1-4

TO BEGIN
Think of the most exciting event in your life. Now try to summarize it as completely as possible in twenty-five words or less. This couple is also having trouble telling an exciting story succinctly.

THE CLIP
Larry (Woody Allen) and Carol Lipton (Diane Keaton) come to believe that their Manhattan neighbor murdered his wife.

In this scene, Larry and Carol try to tell the police that they discovered the body of their murdered neighbor.

FOR DISCUSSION
☞ What unnecessary information are the Liptons giving the police? Why is their task difficult? The Bible tells us how God summarized his plan for humanity in a way that can be understood by all.

☞ What would you ask Microsoft's Bill Gates if he were in this room? Why would you expect him to know the answers? Read the questions about life phrased by Job (3:11-13) and by David (Psalm 6:2, 3 and 10:13). Read Hebrews 1:2. Why would Jesus know the answers?

☞ Imagine being a child lost in a store. What one sight do you want to see above all others? How is that similar to the plights of Moses (Exodus 33:12-18) and of Philip (John 14:1-8)? According to Hebrews 1:3a, how does Jesus provide the last word to those fears?

☞ Read the words of Hebrews 1:3b and 4:16 one after another, forming a single thought. Come to that throne now and ask Jesus, "How can I know that my sins are forgiven?" What does he say?

☞ Divide a sheet of paper into three columns. Place the following headings on them: Questions I have about the things of this world; Questions I have about God's nature and presence; Questions I have about my salvation. Write one or more questions under each column. Read through the Gospel of Mark this week, looking for ways Jesus' ministry answered those questions.

IN CONCLUSION

Jesus is uniquely qualified to authoritatively speak God's message. He can tell us about the things of this world because he owns it, being creator and heir. He can bring us into the presence of God because he radiates it, being in God's exact likeness. He can promise us our salvation because he purchased it with his sacrifice. We can count on Jesus to get God's story straight!

OTHER APPLICATIONS

Use this clip to introduce a sermon, lesson, or devotion on Jesus as the Word of God from John 1:1-18.

INSIDE INFORMATION

Diane Keaton shares a last name with actor Michael Keaton. Not only are they not related, but Keaton is the real name of neither one. Diane was born Diane Hall, a last name she would use in another Woody Allen movie, *Annie Hall* (1977). Michael took his stage name because he admired this actress and the fact that his given name, Michael Douglas, was already used by a popular actor!

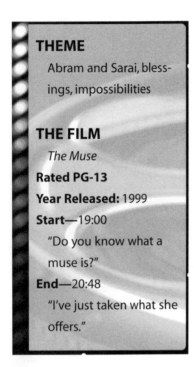

IMPOSSIBLE BLESSINGS
Genesis 17:1-27

TO BEGIN

From magazines, newspapers, direct-mail advertisements, and the Internet, collect advertisements for weight-loss products, dating services, hair-loss remedies, and get-rich-quick schemes. What do they have in common? Why do people try them anyway? Here is someone desperate enough to try anything.

THE CLIP

Down-on-his-luck screenwriter, Steven Phillips (Albert Brooks) enlists the service of Sarah (Sharon Stone), a woman who claims to be a muse from Greek mythology.

In this scene, Steven's friend, journalist Jack Warrick (Jeff Bridges), confesses that his career was saved by a woman he believes to be a daughter of Zeus.

FOR DISCUSSION

⌨ Describe Steven's situation. List reasons why Jack's story is unbelievable. The story of Abram and Sarai is probably just as unbelievable. Yet their story is true.

⌨ Note the name changes mentioned in Genesis 17:1-8, 15, 16. Use Bible reference books (analytic concordance, Bible dictionary, lexicon) to compare the meanings of "Abram" to "Abraham" and "Sarai" to "Sarah." Was the change significant? Explain the remarkable identity changes described in Isaiah 62:1-5, 12; 2 Corinthians 5:14-19; and Revelation 3:11-13. Why do you think

God must change who we are before the impossible starts to happen in our lives?

☞ God's actions don't just break the laws of nature, they shatter them (Ephesians 3:20). Understanding that Abram was just a simple nomad, why was God's promise to him by itself remarkable (Genesis 12:2; 17:4)? Read Genesis 17:17-22. How did Abram suggest God keep his remarkable promise? (Review Genesis 16:1-3, 15 if necessary.) How was God's way of fulfilling the promise more than Abram could ask or imagine? See Genesis 11:30; Romans 4:18, 19; Hebrews 11:11, 12.

☞ A benefactor has just given you a check for one million dollars. Describe every step you now take to actually place that much currency in your hands. Now consider Abram's duty in "cashing" God's promise (Genesis 17:9-14; 23-27). Compare Abram's actions to your endorsing that generous check. Did either action actually earn the blessing? What then is the purpose of our part in keeping God's covenant?

☞ On a single line, write the words of Psalm 37:4. With a scissors, cut the sentence after the word "Lord." Are you satisfied that the last part of that verse has happened? If not, what do you need to do to fulfill the first part of the verse? Carry these two pieces with you this week as you consider ways of putting these phrases together in your life.

IN CONCLUSION

In a world of outrageous claims and seductive offers, it is easy to become cynical. Yet God's blessings can still bring miraculous answers to our desperate situations. As with Abram and Sarai, God's blessings can change who we are, can surpass our wildest dreams, and are accomplished by God's power alone.

OTHER APPLICATIONS

Use this clip to introduce a sermon, lesson, or devotion on the impossible from Hebrews 11:1-6.

INSIDE INFORMATION

The nine muses are Calliope (the muse of epic poetry), Clio (the muse of history), Erato (the muse of love poetry and mimicry), Euterpe (the muse of music), Melpomene (the muse of tragedy), Polyhymnia (the muse of sacred poetry), Terpsichore (muse of dancing), Thalia (the muse of comedy and of playful and idyllic poetry), and Urania (the muse of astronomy).

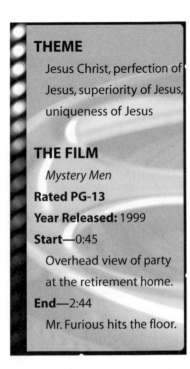

THEME

Jesus Christ, perfection of Jesus, superiority of Jesus, uniqueness of Jesus

THE FILM

Mystery Men

Rated PG-13

Year Released: 1999

Start—0:45

Overhead view of party at the retirement home.

End—2:44

Mr. Furious hits the floor.

JESUS, SO MUCH MORE!

Matthew 12:38-42

TO BEGIN

Fill in these blanks: "I once considered _____ to be a personal hero until _____." Take a look at these heroes that didn't quite live up to expectations.

THE CLIP

Inept superheroes answer the call to save their city.

In this scene, The Blue Raja (Hank Azaria), The Shoveler (William H. Macy), and Mr. Furious (Ben Stiller) are less than super when trying to stop a robbery in a retirement home.

FOR DISCUSSION

☞ Describe the "super powers" of each of these characters. Why do they seem a little disappointing? We laugh, but when we look at our own heroes too closely, we are bound to find that they also are imperfect. What qualities would you expect in a true superhero? While superheroes are products of comic books, the Gospels paint us a picture of a perfect man who is very real.

☞ What did the Pharisees and teachers of the law want in a religious hero (Matthew 12:38, 39a)? Does the performance of miracles alone make a person great? Review Exodus 7:19-23; Matthew 7:15-23; and Revelation 13:11-14. Find miracle workers in those situations who were not true heroes. What was lacking in each case?

✻ When people came into contact with Jesus, they often used a specific title to describe him. Find the common title in Matthew 16:14; Mark 6:15; and John 4:19. To what prophet does Jesus compare himself (Matthew 12:39-41)? Why does he far surpass even this comparison? See Jonah 1:17; 2:10; 1 Corinthians 15:12-20; Ephesians 1:18-21.

✻ Compare 1 Kings 10:1-10 and Matthew 12:42. Why would a comparison to the great King Solomon (son of King David) be a remarkable complement? Defend Jesus' statement that he was greater than Israel's most successful kings. See Acts 2:29-33; 1 Corinthians 15:20-26; and Philippians 2:9-11.

✻ List five or six human beings you admire. Place an A by those whom you admire for their acts of strength, a W by those whom you admire for their words of wisdom, and a P by those who have a position of power and influence. Does anyone on your list have all three? If so, what does Jesus have that even he or she lacks?

IN CONCLUSION

Many people throughout history have led admirable lives. Other religions have prophets and magicians. This world has its great empire builders. But Jesus is so much more!

OTHER APPLICATIONS

Use this clip to introduce a sermon, lesson, or devotion about the uniqueness of Christ from Colossians 1:15-20 or Revelation 5.

OOPS!

A left prosthetic arm is taken off in the robbery but turns into a right arm when it lands in the punch bowl!

35

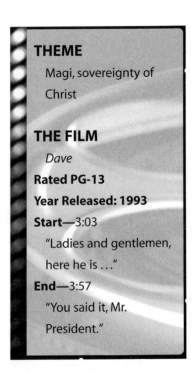

KING OF KINGS
Matthew 2:1-13

TO BEGIN

Have you ever met a celebrity? Whom did you meet? How was this person or situation different than you expected? Let's look at this unusual celebrity encounter.

THE CLIP

Dave Kovic (Kevin Kline), an owner/operator of an employment agency, is called to impersonate the president of the United States.

In this scene, Dave impersonates the president at the grand opening of a car dealership.

FOR DISCUSSION

📽 Repeat the short conversation from this scene between the skeptical young girl and her mother. Expand that conversation to explain what you believe each one meant. The Bible tells us about an even more unusual celebrity appearance. And this one is true!

📽 Look up the word "Magi" in a Bible dictionary. Describe their geographical and religious background. How would you guess that this same word was translated in Acts 13:6, 8? Read Matthew 2:1, 2. Why is it surprising that these "Magi" received such an announcement from God? Does that say anything about the kind of people God continues to call out today? (See 1 Corinthians 6:9-11.)

📽 Survey four or five recent news stories from the

past week about the president of the United States or some other important political figure. Describe the setting of each article. Would you expect the president to be in each of those places? Why or why not? What is unexpected about the setting of the birth of the One superior to all political figures (Matthew 2:6)? Use a Bible dictionary to find out more about this town.

☞ Compare the reception given to the newborn king by his own people (Matthew 2:3, 13) to the reception given to him by foreigners (2:10-12). From what you see there, explain what is meant in John 1:10-13.

☞ Write the words of Luke 19:10 on a note card and memorize it this week. On the back of the note card write the name of two or three people you know who seem unlikely to receive God's message. How can you behave in an unexpected manner toward them this week?

IN CONCLUSION

Jesus' entrance into the world was far from what many expect for the king of all kings. His birth was announced to unexpected people. He was born in an unexpected place. His coming received an unexpected reception. God continues to do the unexpected for those who accept this king today.

OTHER APPLICATIONS

Use this clip to introduce a sermon, lesson, or devotion on the unexpected birth of Christ from Luke 2:1-19.

"SCENE" HER BEFORE?

The skeptical young girl in this scene is Catherine Reitman, daughter of the director, Ivan Reitman. She has appeared in small roles in a number of the director's movies, including *Twins* (1988), *Kindergarten Cop* (1990), and *Fathers' Day* (1997).

THEME

Solomon's wisdom, priorities, values

THE FILM

The First Wives Club

Rated PG

Year Released: 1996

Start—7:24

"Elise, if I give you any more collagen …"

End—8:26

"Fill 'em up."

A KING'S PRIORITIES

1 Kings 3:5-15

TO BEGIN

You have found Aladdin's magic lamp. You are about to rub it and get your three wishes. Reveal one of those wishes now. What wish might the person in this clip make if she found a magic lamp?

THE CLIP

Bren Morelli Cushman (Bette Midler), Elise 'Lisey' Eliot (Goldie Hawn), and Annie MacDuggan Paradis (Diane Keaton) form an informal club of ex-wives after being dumped by their husbands for "newer models."

In this scene Elise begs her plastic surgeon (Rob Reiner) to make her look younger.

FOR DISCUSSION

🎥 Describe Elise's wish. What are some reasons for her wish? Is this a common priority for many? Why do you believe that to be so? The Bible tells about a king who had a very different wish for his life.

🎥 One of the world's wealthiest men was once asked, "How much wealth is enough?" The man replied, "Just a little more." Imagine responses that Solomon (1 Kings 3:5, 6) and Paul (1 Timothy 6:6-8) might make to that question. Would Solomon and Paul agree? What would they say?

🎥 React to this statement: "Our biggest need today is not having more wealth, but rather having the ability to use the wealth we have." Paraphrase 1 Corinthians 4:2 as simply as you can. How do Solomon's words (1 Kings 3:7-9) indicate that he understood this truth that Paul would later state?

☜ Compare the promise made to Solomon (1 Kings 3:10-15) with its fulfillment (1 Kings 10:14-29). How does Ephesians 3:20 seem to apply to Solomon's blessings?

☜ Create a priority report card for yourself on a sheet of paper. Grade yourself on these subjects: Recognition of and thankfulness for blessings received; Desire to care for that which God makes me responsible; Watching expectantly for further blessings from God. For which would you receive the lowest grade? What make-up work can you do to bring your grade up?

IN CONCLUSION

We can learn a lot from Solomon when we set priorities in our lives. First, Solomon was grateful for the blessings he had. Then, Solomon's highest priority was to fulfill the responsibilities God had given him. And though Solomon did not consider his personal comfort as a priority, God allowed him to have that as well. How well do our goals meet those standards?

OTHER APPLICATIONS

Use this clip to introduce a sermon, lesson, or devotion on setting priorities from Matthew 25:14-30 or Luke 12:35-48.

INSIDE INFORMATION

The three actresses staring in this movie were all born within a month and a half of each other: Hawn on November 21, 1945; Midler on December 1, 1945; and Keaton on January 5, 1946. They each celebrated their fiftieth birthday while making this film.

THEME

burning bush, communication from God

THE FILM

L. A. Story

Rated PG-13

Year Released: 1991

Start—20:00

"There are two events in my life I consider to be magical."

End—22:40

"You talkin' to signs, you are in trouble."

A MESSAGE FROM GOD
Exodus 3:1-10

TO BEGIN

Look in your local phone book's yellow pages under "Telegrams—Singing and Novelty." How many businesses are listed for your area? Why would people choose such unusual ways to send a message? Note this unusual messenger.

THE CLIP

Harris Telemacher (Steve Martin), the "Wacky Weather Man" for a Los Angeles television station, tries to find happiness and purpose despite his chaotic West Coast lifestyle.

After his car stalls on the freeway, Harris is greeted by a signpost.

FOR DISCUSSION

☞ Describe the message and the messenger in this scene. As strange as this scene is, an account from biblical history is even stranger.

☞ What extremely unusual characteristic of the burning bush drew Moses' attention to it (Exodus 3:1-5)? Consider the image for a moment. What action of God does fire usually symbolize (Matthew 5:22; 2 Peter 3:7)? What does a bush preserved though surrounded by fire tell us about God's plans for his people (Daniel 3:17; 1 John 4:16-18)?

☞ How did God describe his purpose for appearing to Moses (Exodus 3:6-9)? What do you think God meant when he said, "And now the cry of the Israelites have reached me" (v. 9)? Considering God's words to Abram centuries before (Genesis 15:12-16), do you think that he literally meant that the matter just came to his attention? Compare Genesis 15:16 and 2 Peter 3:9. Why do God's plans sometimes take time?

🎥 Read Exodus 3:10. If God could speak to Moses through a burning bush, why do you think he didn't speak directly to Pharaoh in this way? Does God continue to use human messengers today (2 Corinthians 5:18-20). Examine the apostle Paul's explanation for God's use of human messengers (2 Corinthians 4:5-7). Can you paraphrase Paul's explanation without using his symbolic language?

🎥 God is calling you now. Which of these best applies to your reception: 1. "Sorry, I'm out right now. Please leave a message"; 2. "I'll get on it immediately"; 3. "Too much static, the call is breaking up"; or 4. "Sorry, wrong number"?

IN CONCLUSION

No stranger sign than the burning bush can be seen in fact or fiction! Yet there is also none more meaningful. A bush that burned without being consumed clearly pictures a God whose primary task is redemption, not destruction. God's call on behalf of his people displays his faithfulness in keeping his promises. Finally, his call to Moses demonstrates that God works through servants he chooses.

OTHER APPLICATIONS
Use this clip to introduce a sermon, lesson, or devotion about a message from God from Luke 1:26-38.

"SCENE" HER BEFORE?
Marilu Henner, best known as Elaine Nardo in the TV series "Taxi," plays Harris's companion Trudi.

THEME
love, sacrifice, service

THE FILM
Splash
Rated PG
Year Released: 1984
Start—1:24:22
"Oh, Oh Mr. Bauer, you had a million messages."
End—1:25:25
"Nobody said love's perfect."

NO GREATER LOVE
John 15:9-17

TO BEGIN

Pretend that you are four years old. In that role, complete the sentence: "I love _____." Restate the sentence without using the word "love." Repeat that exercise as a ten-year-old, a sixteen-year-old, and at your present age.

"Love" is a word that we have used all of our lives. Yet we never seem to have a complete understanding of it. Remember this clip of someone confused by what he thought was love?

THE CLIP

Allen Bauer (Tom Hanks) meets and falls in love with Madison (Daryl Hannah), the girl of his dreams. Then he discovers that she is a mermaid.

In this scene, Allen complains to his brother Freddie (John Candy) that love wasn't what he had hoped it would be.

FOR DISCUSSION

☞ How has Allen's view of love changed within hours? What is the relationship between love and knowledge of a person? Consider Freddie's advice. How satisfying of an answer does he give? Explain. In his last days with his disciples, Jesus provided a clear picture of what love is.

☞ Read John 15:9, 10 and Exodus 19:3-6. What element is essential to love that lasts? Give examples of how refusing to acknowledge the wishes of another can destroy a love relationship.

☞ Tell of the time you were the happiest with some-one you loved. How was mutual obedience dis-played in that relationship? Why is "complete joy" a good description of your state at that time? (See John 15:11; 1 John 1:3, 4.)

☞ Defend this statement: "Childish love is a feeling, but mature love is a commitment to action and to partnership." (See John 15:13-17; Philippians 2:4-8.)

☞ Draw a line on a piece of paper. Label one end "childish love" and the other "mature love." Plot at least three of your relationships along that line. What specific actions could you take to move those relationships toward maturity?

IN CONCLUSION

What often passes for love is simply selfishness. Mature love submits, sacrifices, and brings mutual joy and fulfilling partnership.

OTHER APPLICATIONS

Use this clip to intro-duce a sermon, lesson, or devotion on sacrificial love from any of these texts: Hosea 11; Mark 10:42-45; John 3:16, 17.

INSIDE INFORMATION

Early in their respec-tive careers actor Tom Hanks and director Ron Howard made a suc-cessful team in this comedy. More than a decade later, they would reunite as a much more seasoned actor and director in the powerful drama, *Apollo 13* (1995).

THEME
Ezra, going home with
God, return to Jerusalem

THE FILM
Home Alone
Rated PG
Year Released: 1990
Start—1:03:47
"Santa, hold on!"
End—1:05:00
"I won't. Thanks"

RETURN

Ezra 1

TO BEGIN
What did you most want for Christmas at the age of seven? seventeen? twenty-one? Compare those gifts. What effect has your maturity had on what you consider important? Consider this Christmas wish.

THE CLIP
Kevin McCallister (Macaulay Culkin) is an eight-year-old boy who is accidentally left at home by his parents when they leave for a Christmas vacation.

Kevin asks Santa (Ken Campbell) for his family's return for Christmas.

FOR DISCUSSION
☞ What was Kevin's wish? What more childish desires did it override? Was there any time in your life when being home with family would have been the best present you could have received? After about seven decades of exile, going home was the great longing of Israel. And that gift would be delivered.

☞ In 587 B.C., Nebuchadnezzar of Babylon attacked Jerusalem, destroyed the temple, and took the residents of the city captive. In the decades that followed, Persia conquered Babylon. Summarize the events of Ezra 1:1-3. Compare them to the words of Jeremiah who wrote seven decades before Ezra 1 (Jeremiah 25:8-12; 29:10, 11) and the words of Isaiah who prophesied more than a century before that (Isaiah 44:24-28; 45:13). What can you surmise about God's ability to fulfill our desires?

🖙 Imagine that you have just decided to secede from the country. You announce that you are no longer subject to the laws of your government. What effect would that have on the authority your government has over you? Explain. The people of Persia (including Cyrus) were not Jews nor did they claim allegiance to Jehovah. Did that affect the amount of authority Jehovah actually had over them? Explain, referring to Ezra 1:2-4, 6 and Isaiah 45:1-6.

🖙 God planned the release of his people from captivity. He further influenced those who did not worship him (Cyrus and the Persians) to allow for this event to happen and be financed. Yet what was still necessary for the return to happen (Ezra 1:5)? How can we likewise be prepared for the blessings God has in store for us? See Hebrews 3:12-15.

🖙 Note that we will be called to go home with God one day. Meditate on the words of Revelation 19:6-8 daily this week. Make a "to do" list in preparation for this event. You have a trip to plan!

IN CONCLUSION

A generation of God's people longed for the day when they would return to their homeland. That day came in God's timing. Even those who were thought of as the enemies of God's people were enlisted by God to bring about that day. And on that day, God's prepared people were ready to receive that promise. Their desire to be home again was granted.

OTHER APPLICATIONS

Use this clip to introduce a sermon, lesson, or devotion on going home with God from 1 Thessalonians 4:13–5:11.

"SCENE" HIM BEFORE?

Though you can't place the face, does Santa's voice sound strangely familiar? Ken Hudson Campbell supplied the voice of Bob the baby on the series of TV commercials for freeinternet.com in the year 2000.

45

REWARDS OF INTEGRITY

Genesis 6:5-22

TO BEGIN

White House aide George Stephanopolous appeared on "Larry King Live" during the first term of the Clinton administration, and said, "The president has kept all of the promises he intended to keep." Have you ever made a promise you never intended to keep? Perhaps it may have been one like this.

THE CLIP

Virtuous police officer Charlie Lang (Nicolas Cage) promises to split his lottery winnings with down-on-her-luck waitress Yvonne Biasi (Bridget Fonda) in lieu of a tip.

In this scene, Charlie returns to keep his promise.

FOR DISCUSSION

☞ Do you believe Charlie thought he would have to keep his original promise? Explain. Why do you think he returned to Yvonne anyway? The Bible tells us about Noah, a man who had integrity, even though it was far from easy to do so.

☞ Find a food product with a label that boasts, "all natural ingredients." Why is that generally considered to be desirable? On the other hand, can you list things found in nature that you would never want to find in that food product? Is a person who has "all natural ingredients" appetizing to God (Romans 8:5-8)? How is that exemplified in the people of Noah's day (Genesis 6:5-7)?

☞ Read the words of Jesus in Matthew 7:13, 14. Why are Jesus' words especially apt in describing Noah's plight (Genesis 6:5-10)? Imagine some adjustments and struggles Noah must have had to make in order to keep "on the road." Why does the information contained in verse 10 make it even more important that Noah lived with integrity?

☞ Ultimately Noah had to rely upon God to escape the depravity of the world (Genesis 6:11-22). What does that say about our ability to save ourselves? What (actually "who") is God's lifeboat for us? How do we get on board? See 1 Peter 3:18-22.

☞ Read Matthew 24:36-44. How is our day like the days of Noah? How do we prepare for the trip that we may take at any time? Make three lists of character traits, habits, and personal goals this week under these headings: "Essentials for the trip"; "Those things I'll pack if I have room"; and "Throw them overboard!"

IN CONCLUSION

Noah shows that even when the world is overwhelmingly against us, it is possible to live with integrity. Furthermore, we see that God rewards one who will withstand the call of his fallen nature and heed the call of the Spirit.

OTHER APPLICATIONS

Use this clip to introduce a sermon, lesson, or devotion on integrity from Philippians 4:4-9 or 1 Peter 2:11-17.

INSIDE INFORMATION

In 1997 Bridget Fonda was offered the title role of the TV series "Ally McBeal" (1997), but turned it down without even reading the script.

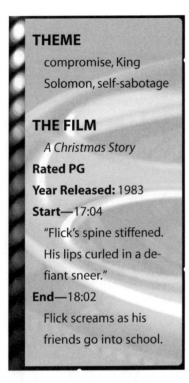

SELF-SABOTAGE

1 Kings 11:1-40

TO BEGIN

Take a piece of duct tape approximately one foot in length. Fold the middle six inches of the tape so the sticky sides meet, leaving about three inches of tape on either side. Have two members of the group grasp those two ends and try to pull the folded section apart. Here is a clip of someone else in a sticky situation.

THE CLIP

Ralphie Parker (Peter Billingsley) experiences highs and lows of the Christmas season as a child in the 1940's.

On a dare from his friend Schwartz (R. D. Robb), Flick (Scott Schwartz) puts his tongue on a cold flagpole with predictable results.

FOR DISCUSSION

☛ List some thoughts Flick probably had the moment he realized he was stuck. Although he was challenged by his peers to perform this stunt, who really was to blame for his plight? Although different in almost every way from this character, King Solomon of Israel would have had to make the same admission.

☛ In ancient days it was not unusual for a king or prince to marry a royal woman of a rival nation to form an alliance between the nations. But since Israel was to rely on God alone for safety, what would be the implication of this practice if a king of Israel were to do it (1 Kings 11:1, 2)? What eventually happened because of this lack of faith (vv. 3-13)? As Christians we must find our security in God and in those institutions he has created for us—the church and the family. Do you see a similarity between Solomon's promiscuity and sexual promiscuity for the Christian today (1 Corinthians 6:12-20)?

☞ If national security was a reason for Solomon's polygamy, was it successful? Who were Hadad and Rezon? Describe the international intrigue that threatened Israel from outside her borders (1 Kings 11:14-25).

☞ Did Solomon's polygamy cause domestic problems as well (1 Kings 11:26-40)? Summarize the prophecy of Ahijah. What would be the ultimate result of Solomon's faithlessness?

☞ On the palm of your hand with a washable marker, write a problem that you have been making worse (and even compromising your values) by trying to handle it yourself. After the group dismisses, wash that hand thoroughly, praying as you do so that God will give you the faith to release the situation to him.

IN CONCLUSION

Solomon was his own worst enemy when he was unfaithful to Jehovah God. As a result, he was stuck. Both foreign adversaries and internal rebellion threatened to destroy one of the wealthiest, most stable empires in history.

OTHER APPLICATIONS

Use this clip to introduce a sermon, lesson, or devotion on compromise from 2 Chronicles 16.

"SCENE" IT BEFORE?

The format of this film, narration of childhood memories by the main character as an adult, was used in the popular television program, "The Wonder Years" (1988-1993).

THEME
Faith, walking on water

THE FILM
As Good As It Gets
Rated PG-13
Year Released: 1997
Start—34:17
"I think it's a beautiful day for our walk today."
End—35:10
"Let's go home and do some writing."

STEPS OF FAITH
Matthew 14:22-33

TO BEGIN
Complete this sentence: "Anyone who knows me would say that the weirdest habit or mannerism I have is _____." Look at how this one man's habits were noticed and mimicked by another.

THE CLIP
Obsessive-compulsive writer Melvin Udall (Jack Nicholson) becomes a better person because of Carol Connelly (Helen Hunt), a single mother who works as a waitress.

In this scene, Melvin takes his neighbor's dog for a walk and notices that the dog has picked up some of his own obsessive-compulsive ways.

FOR DISCUSSION
🎥 Watch the dog as he follows Melvin. Notice how they both react to cracks in the sidewalk. Play the clip again if you missed it. I'm sure God doesn't care if we step on sidewalk cracks. The Bible does, however, tell us about other steps he wants us to take.

🎥 Find the common quote of Jesus in Matthew 14:22-27; Matthew 17:5-8; and Mark 5:21-36. Why was Jesus feared in each of these situations? Look at the last two words of Jesus' answer in Mark 5:36. In what way is faith the opposite of fear in each of these situations?

🎥 Find the common command of Jesus in Matthew

14:28, 29; Matthew 11:28-30; and Matthew 19:13, 14. Who are being called? What do they have in common? Why is it significant that Jesus is a king who calls the weak and powerless?

☞ Find the common action of Jesus in Matthew 14:30-33 and in Matthew 8:1-3. What did he accomplish by this act in each case? Compare Deuteronomy 5:15 to these two verses. Despite our failing faith, what does our God continually desire to do?

☞ Make a list of things you know you should be doing in your life. What is keeping you from completing these tasks? Place a F by any item that you are simply afraid to do. Place a P by those items that are not getting done because you feel powerless (lacking time, finances, or another resource) to complete. Place a 2 by items that you have tried but need God's strength to try again. Read the account in Matthew 14:22-33 every day this week and review this list. Pray for strength in accomplishing at least one task.

IN CONCLUSION

Jesus knows that the walk of faith to which he calls us is frightening. He welcomes us, nevertheless, to take those steps, and his steadying hand is available when our faith fails and our eyes stray from him. Instead of copying the superstitious walk of Melvin, let's take the bold steps of Peter!

OTHER APPLICATIONS

Use this clip to introduce a sermon, lesson, or devotion on stepping out on faith from Hebrews 11.

INSIDE INFORMATION

For this scene, the dog was taught not to step on cracks by putting obstacles in front of him. The obstacles were removed electronically, giving the impression that he was avoiding "back-breaking" consequences.

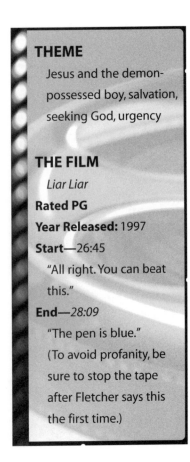

URGENT BUSINESS
Mark 9:14-24

TO BEGIN

Shake a can of soda for all to see. Then offer it to a member of the group. Everyone will be hesitant to open it because the can will not be able to contain its contents. Have you ever felt like that? Or like this?

THE CLIP

Sleazy attorney Fletcher Reede (Jim Carrey) finds that he cannot tell a lie.

In this scene, no matter how hard he tries to suppress it, the truth comes out of Fletcher's mouth and pen.

FOR DISCUSSION

⛟ How strong was the outside compulsion for Fletcher to tell the truth? How was that illustrated here? In the book of Mark, Jesus comes upon a situation that urgently needed God's power. Three times the word "straightway" (KJV), meaning "immediately" or "with urgency," is used.

⛟ Read Mark 9:14-19; Acts 2:29-37; and Acts 16:25-30. Each of these passages describes a person or people in urgent need. Describe those people and those situations. How are their needs and situations similar and how do they differ? What common step did each take in dealing with an urgent need?

⛟ Agree or disagree: "Education is the answer.

Ignorance, and ignorance alone, is the power that causes and prolongs human suffering." Refer to Mark 9:20-22; Romans 1:18; 2 Corinthians 4:4; and Ephesians 6:12 as you compose your response. Describe the forces that urgently resist truth and mercy in each case.

How was the offer of God's grace responded to in Mark 9:23, 24? Take a look at a coupon, a carton of milk, and your driver's license. Each has a date on it with similar significance. What is it? Why is it unwise to ignore an expiration date in any of these cases? Summarize God's advice about responding to his offer of grace (Acts 2:38-40; 2 Corinthians 5:20–6:2; Ephesians 5:15, 16).

Consider these commands: Seek solutions. Fight evil. Accept grace. Of these three messages, do you believe God wishes you to urgently respond to one of them in particular? Which one? What specific response does God want you to make?

IN CONCLUSION

The battle for the salvation of mankind is one of greatest urgency. Those who recognize their fallen state urgently search for answers. Satan desperately tries to keep them from finding salvation. Therefore when one learns of the good news, it is wise to respond decisively. It needs to be truth that just can't be denied!

OTHER APPLICATIONS

Use this clip to introduce a sermon, lesson, or devotion on urgency from Romans 12:1, 2; 2 Corinthians 6:1, 2; or Ephesians 4:1-3.

INSIDE INFORMATION

Since this film, stuntman Pat Banta has been the personal stunt double for Jim Carrey.

THEME

   battling evil, David and
   Goliath, victory

THE FILM

   It Happened One Night

Not Rated

Year Released: 1934

Start—1:00:44

   "Suppose nobody stops
   for us, huh?"

End—1:03:37

   Car screeches to a halt.

VICTORY, GOD'S WAY
1 Samuel 17:20-50

TO BEGIN

Divide into groups to play ticktacktoe. Describe your strategy for playing the game. Consider the strategies for another venture described here.

THE CLIP

Spoiled heiress Ellie Andrews (Claudette Colbert) escapes from her domineering father and reluctantly accepts the help of out-of-work reporter Peter Warner (Clark Gable).

In this well-known scene, Ellie and Peter use different strategies for hitchhiking.

FOR DISCUSSION

☞ What do you think of Peter's hitchhiking strategies? Are they logical? Might they work in some situations? Why or why not? In the familiar story of David and Goliath, we can discern a strategy for a much more serious venture—the business of defeating evil.

☞ MOTIVE—What motives usually start conflicts (James 4:1-3)? Can you think of examples? Imagine the thoughts going through David's mind as he approached the battlefield (1 Samuel 17:20-30). Reread verse 26. What two motives for doing battle with Goliath seemed to be foremost on David's mind? Which one of these seems to take first place in the minds of the others (vv. 25, 27, 30)? Compare the other motive to attitudes a more mature David expressed later in his life (Psalm 2).

METHODS—Read 1 Samuel 17:31-40. Summarize the disagreements between David and Saul. What methods did each deem necessary to defeat Goliath? What prompted David's choice of weapons? How does his choice agree with the understanding of gifts Paul explains in Ephesians 4:7, 8, 12?

MASTER—Finish reading this story (1 Samuel 17:41-50). Underline the words of David. Support this statement from those words: "When one wars against evil, the battle is about the power of God, not the reputation of the warrior." In what non-violent ways do we battle evil so that the world will know our Master (John 13:34, 35; 17:20-23)?

Is there a giant harassing you? Have you gotten angry with him for challenging God's authority, or do you merely feel inconvenienced? Are you using your unique abilities to defeat him or are you too busy trying on another hero's armor?

OTHER APPLICATIONS

Use this clip to introduce a sermon, lesson, or devotion on victory over evil from 2 Chronicles 20:1-30.

INSIDE INFORMATION

The carrot munching in this scene was the inspiration for Bugs Bunny's mannerisms in the famous Warner Brothers cartoons.

IN CONCLUSION

David's experience provides a model for battling evil. He was motivated by his anger towards evil and those who mocked his God. He used methods that were compatible with the gifts he knew he had. Finally, he never lost sight of his Master, fighting for the glory of God rather than personal goals.

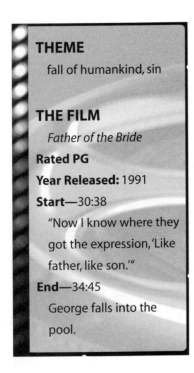

THE WAGES OF SIN

Genesis 3:1-24

TO BEGIN

Gather your group in a circle. Start by saying: "I woke up one morning and thought I could relax and do nothing all day. *But then* I realized that I had forgotten to mail a check that needed to go out that day. I grabbed the bill, *but then* . . ." Have the person on your right continue the story, describing the next negative turn the day would take. Each person should end with the words, "but then" and have the next person continue. After your story is complete, show this other example of how life can go from bad to worse.

THE CLIP

George and Nina Banks (Steve Martin and Diane Keaton) prepare for their daughter's wedding.

In this scene George falls prey to the temptation to explore his future in-laws house, yielding disastrous results.

FOR DISCUSSION

🎦 Try to list the disasters visited upon George in this clip. When did they begin? At what point could he have made a decision to stop them? The Bible tells us about a single decision that has consequences to this day.

🎦 Which of these statements is the most true for you: "I wish I could be in the presence of God" or "I wish I could hide from God's sight"? Are they sometimes both true? Explain how they were both true for Adam and Eve (Genesis 3:8-10, 22-24). Can you think of ways that this love-hate relationship with God shows in the lives of people today?

☞ List social problems today that are at least in part sexual in nature (for example, divorce, loneliness, abortion, pornography, sexual abuse). Describe the sexual climate of the garden before this event (Genesis 2:18-25). Looking at the results of the fall listed in 3:7, 12, and 16, discuss how they caused that sexual climate to change and perhaps led to some of the problems we face today.

☞ What do you think Paul meant by the words of Romans 8:22? How do the events of Genesis 3:17-19 describe this "groaning"?

☞ Consider the three separations caused by sin: separation from God, separation from one another, and separation from nature. On a sheet of paper, create a symbol to represent a symptom of one or more of those separations in your life. During this week, look at that picture while you meditate upon Romans 8:23-28, asking God to allow "the firstfruits of the Spirit" to ease that separation.

IN CONCLUSION

Though placed in the paradise of Eden, Adam and Eve decided to disobey God. From that point on, life went from bad to worse. From that point on, sin began to separate us from God, from each other, and even from the natural processes in the world.

OTHER APPLICATIONS

Use this clip to introduce a sermon, lesson, or devotion on sin from Romans 3:9-24.

INSIDE INFORMATION

Stanley Kubrick liked Steve Martin's work in *The Jerk* (1979) and once considered having him play Bill Harford in *Eyes Wide Shut* (1999), the role that later went to Tom Cruise.

THEME
Joshua entering promised land, success

THE FILM
Picture Perfect
Rated PG-13
Year Released: 1997
Start—3:04
Boardroom doors are shut.
End—5:23
"And that ain't bad."
(To avoid vulgarity, stop tape immediately.)

WE'RE NUMBER ONE!
Joshua 1:1-18

TO BEGIN

How many U.S. presidents can you name? Now try to name as many vice presidents. Why do you think one list is longer than the other? What might that say about the truth of this clip?

THE CLIP

Kate Mosley (Jennifer Aniston) is working on a career at Mercer Advertising, but finds her personal and professional lives uncomfortably intertwined.

In this scene, Kate presents an idea for an advertising campaign for a famous mustard.

FOR DISCUSSION

☞ What slogan did Kate suggest? Do you believe that a company would be content to remain number two? Explain. As they entered the promised land, Joshua and the people of Israel were not content with second place. God told Joshua how to have complete success.

☞ Note the command that is repeated in Joshua 1:6, 7a, 9, 18. Consider great heroes of both fact and fiction. In what ways did they obey this command? What are some factors that contributed to their courage? Try to explain the relationship between faith in God and courage (Joshua 1:9; Philippians 1:27, 28).

☞ Have you ever told someone to "put it in writing"? Why did you say it? What did you mean by it? In what way was the confidence and courage of the Israelites strengthened by a "written contract" with God? Did they have obligations under the contract? See Joshua 1:7b, 8.

🎥 A common nightmare is being back in school and finding that you have to take a test that you forgot about. Have you had this or a similar nightmare? Note how the command in Joshua 1:11 addresses such fear. The word translated "get . . . ready" is the Hebrew word *kun*. Guess how that same word is translated in 1 Kings 2:12; Proverbs 12:3; 16:12; 25:4, 5. Note that getting ready (or "being established") has moral implications. See also Matthew 7:24-27 and 1 Corinthians 3:10-13.

🎥 The American armed services has used the slogan, "Be all you can be," for recruitment. If God sent you to boot camp right now to prepare you to fulfill that goal, in which of these pursuits would you be assigned to spend the most time: Strength training to toughen up? Studying the field manual for proper behavior? War games to practice applying what you know? Explain.

IN CONCLUSION

We must never settle for being less than all God wants us to be. Yet to be all we can be is not easy. We must show strength and courage based upon our faith in God who loves us. We must remain obedient to the will of God revealed to us. We must prepare ourselves by living lives characterized by doing what is right.

OTHER APPLICATIONS

Use this clip to introduce a sermon, lesson, or devotion on success from 1 John 5:1-5.

OOPS!

Though it makes a good story, Cindy Crawford did not graduate second in her college class. She was valedictorian of her DeKalb (Illinois) High School graduating class and also received a scholarship to study chemical engineering at Northwestern (Illinois) University. She attended only one semester at Northwestern, however.

THEME

Cain and Abel, conflict

THE FILM

White Christmas

Not Rated

Year Released: 1954

Start—20:23

"Ladies and gentlemen, the Haynes sisters."

End—22:28

Applause.

CONFLICT IN THE FAMILY
Genesis 4:2-16

TO BEGIN

Complete this thought: "I remember the time when my brother/sister . . ." Was it a positive or negative experience? How did it compare to the story of these siblings?

THE CLIP

Two song and dance men (Bing Crosby and Danny Kaye) join with a sister act (Rosemary Clooney and Vera-Ellen) for a holiday show in a Vermont inn.

In this scene, the Haynes sisters perform their famous theme song.

FOR DISCUSSION

☞ What are some positive aspects of Betty and Judy's relationship? How were those shown? What problems could arise in their relationship? Explain. The Bible tells a story of the ultimate sibling rivalry.

☞ Try to identify with some of the feelings experienced by Cain in Genesis 4:2-5. Toward whom were his negative feelings directed? Why do you believe he was feeling that way? Imagine that Cain was then given the "prescription" found in 1 Peter 2:1-3 to deal with those feelings. If Cain followed those commands, what specific actions might he have taken?

☞ Read Genesis 4:6-9. Turn to James 4:1-6. Slightly rewrite the words of James, inserting Cain's name and other appropriate references to create a possible response from God to Cain's question. Reread Genesis 4:6-9, following it with your rewritten response.

🔲 It is said that four of the great themes of literature are a character's conflict with nature, conflict with himself, conflict with God, and conflict with others. Look at the results of Cain's rivalry with Abel in Genesis 4:10-13. Find each of those areas of conflict in those verses.

🔲 On a strip of paper create a scale on which to rate your relationships. Draw a line the width of the paper. Label the left end "harmony." About one quarter of the length of the line from the left make a mark and label it "envy." Label a halfway point "indifference." At about one quarter of the length from the right label a point "hatred." Label the extreme right end "total alienation." Consider five individuals that are siblings, other family members, or brothers or sisters in Christ. Where do your relationships stand on this scale? This week, select one of them and vow to make steps of restoration in that relationship.

IN CONCLUSION

Envy can be the source of sibling conflict (Genesis 4:2-5). Such conflict can grow into indifference and even hatred (vv. 6-9). When that happens, families suffer for generations (vv. 10-13). May the Lord help us strengthen our relationships with our brothers and sisters!

OTHER APPLICATIONS

Use this clip to introduce a sermon, lesson, or devotion on family conflict from Genesis 27:41-45 or Genesis 37:12-36.

"SCENE" HER BEFORE?

Fans of TV's "ER" may remember Rosemary Clooney's guest appearance as Madame X on the program's first Christmas episode, "The Gift." She appeared in the episode with her nephew, George Clooney.

THEME
confronting a problem,
Joseph and Mary

THE FILM
The Sound of Music
Not Rated
Year Released: 1965
Start—9:49
"Well, Reverend
Mother…"
End—14:13
"How do you hold a moon-
beam in your hand?"

FACING A PROBLEM
Matthew 1:18-25

TO BEGIN

Which answer best describes you? "When I have a problem with someone, I usually A) face it head-on and let the chips fall where they may; B) take time to consider a well-thought-out plan; C) ignore it and hope it goes away; or D) blame myself and try to make it right." Have you ever just sung about it? (An unusual approach, granted!)

THE CLIP

Sister Maria (Julie Andrews) becomes the new governess for the children of widower Captain von Trapp (Christopher Plummer).

In this scene, the nuns of the convent musically ponder the fate of their troublesome novice.

FOR DISCUSSION

🎬 Why was Maria a problem? Do you get the sense that the nuns feel a little ambivalent about their anger? The Bible tells about someone who was not quite sure what to do with another problem called "Mary."

🎬 Describe the problem with Mary that was brought to Joseph's attention (Matthew 1:18, 19). Do you find the language describing Joseph's discovery of the situation a bit strange? What is *not* mentioned in these verses that should be a part of problem resolution (Matthew 18:15)? Circle the word "considered" in Matthew 1:20. This Greek word *enthumethentos* comes from the Greek words *en* and *thumos.* Look up these words in a lexicon and try to describe Joseph's mental state in your own words. What is a logical first step in dealing with problems?

☞ What steps did God take to make sure Joseph had correct information (Matthew 1:20-23)? What possible reactions could Joseph have had to this message? What should we do when we wonder if God is trying to tell us something (1 Thessalonians 5:19-21)?

☞ Finish reading this account (Matthew 1:24, 25). You are in the locker room of the Nazareth gym shortly after these events occurred. Relate some of the gossip you overhear there. What did Joseph risk to obey God? What could he have chosen to do to avoid or mitigate some of these problems? What might Solomon have said about Joseph's actions (Proverbs 11:3, 13; 20:19)?

☞ Write the words of Matthew 5:9 on a card and memorize it this week. Ask God to direct you to someone with whom you need to make peace. Follow the three steps discovered in this lesson.

IN CONCLUSION

"What do you do with a problem like Maria" (Mary)? From this story we see the advantage of getting accurate information directly, listening to God for direction, and obeying God without regard to personal distress.

OTHER APPLICATIONS

Use this clip to introduce a sermon, lesson, or devotion on problem solving from Matthew 18:15-20 or 1 Corinthians 6:1-8.

INSIDE INFORMATION

Mary Martin, who originated the role of Maria on Broadway and coproduced the film, would eventually see nearly $80,000,000 from the film. In contrast Julie Andrews earned just $225,000 for her performance.

THEME

Apostasy, deception, doctrine, false teachers

THE FILM

The Wiz

Rated G

Year Released: 1978

Start—28:33

"Succulent and divine!"

End—34:15

"You can't get out of the game."

FACING FALSE TEACHERS
2 Corinthians 11:1-20

TO BEGIN

Construct a short story or conversation that ends with the line, "Trust me. I'm looking out for you here." Who speaks that line in your story? Would it be wise to trust that character? How is your story similar to this one?

THE CLIP

Dorothy (Diana Ross) seeks the help of the Wiz (Richard Pryor) in this urban musical adaptation of *The Wizard of Oz*.

In this scene, the scarecrow (Michael Jackson) is tormented by the crows that rob his field and keep him captive.

FOR DISCUSSION

☞ Do the crows intend to help the scarecrow? What is their goal? Although we want to think the best of people, sometimes we need to be perspicacious (careful). Paul taught the church in Corinth how to spot charlatans who came into that congregation.

☞ Write these two headings on the board: "Impressive Presentation" and "Inadequate Content." As a group, read 2 Corinthians 11:1-6; Matthew 7:15; 23:2; and 2 Timothy 4:3, 4. Put words or phrases from each of those passages into the appropriate column. Defend this statement: "False teachers stress presentation over content."

☝ How did Paul's reason for preaching distinguish him from religious con men (2 Corinthians 11:7-12)? Compare Paul's attitude to that of Jesus. See Mark 10:41-45; Luke 22:24-27; and Philippians 2:5-8. Defend this statement, "False teachers are more concerned with making a living than with sharing eternal life."

☝ Consider this statement: "False teachers enslave rather than liberate." Summarize the content of 2 Corinthians 11:13-20; Jeremiah 20:1, 2; Ezekiel 34:1-4; and Matthew 23:4, 13. How do each of these support that statement?

☝ Consider the "towel test" in evaluating a leader. Read John 13:3-5, 12-14. What towel of servant-hood has Jesus handed some leaders you know? Have they been faithful in that task? What about you?

THE CONCLUSION

False teachers focus on presentation to deceive others into providing them with wealth and power. Godly teachers, on the other hand, preach truth in order to free others with God's good news.

OTHER APPLICATIONS

Use this clip to introduce a sermon, lesson, or devotion about false teachers from Acts 20:28-31; Galatians 1:6-10; Philippians 3:1-4, 17-19; Colossians 2:6-19; 2 Timothy 3:1-9; 2 Peter 2; 1 John 4:1-6; or Jude 3-16.

INSIDE INFORMATION

This blockbuster musical failed miserably at the box office, bringing in barely half of its twenty-four-million-dollar budget. Many attribute its failure to a negative perception of G rated movies in the 1970s.

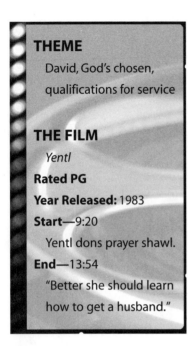

THEME

David, God's chosen, qualifications for service

THE FILM

Yentl

Rated PG

Year Released: 1983

Start—9:20

Yentl dons prayer shawl.

End—13:54

"Better she should learn how to get a husband."

GOD'S CHOSEN
1 Samuel 16:1-13

TO BEGIN

Do you think that people sometimes make false judgments about you because of your appearance or some other superficial reason? On an adhesive label briefly describe your true contents that some may overlook. Wear it proudly, explain it, and then watch this clip.

THE CLIP

A Jewish girl named Yentl (Barbra Streisand) disguises herself as a boy in order to study the Talmud formally.

In this scene, Yentl sings, questioning restrictions put upon her relationship with God because she is a woman.

FOR DISCUSSION

☙ What discrimination did Yentl face? What makes a person qualified to serve God? One of the Bible's greatest leaders was almost passed over for leadership. Let's examine that event.

☙ When you were dating, did you ever dismiss a potential companion by saying, "He/She is not my type"? After a relationship did not work out, did you ever seek another person of the same type? Israel had been jilted by King Saul. Note Samuel's emotional reaction to Saul's betrayal (1 Samuel 15:35–16:1). Review the type Samuel believed would make a good king (1 Samuel 9:1, 2). Read 1 Samuel 16:1-7a. How did Samuel's prejudices about what a king should be affect his judgment?

🎬 Fill in the blank: "I don't know if I would be comfortable hiring a _____ who was younger than I am." Explain your feelings. What evidence do you see that Jesse had some age requirements in mind for the position of king (1 Samuel 16:8-11)? Do the characteristics of age and maturity always coincide? Explain how you would go about differentiating between the age and the maturity of a leader (1 Timothy 4:12-16).

🎬 Explain how God judges potential leaders (1 Samuel 13:14; 16:7b). Saul had the heart of a warrior (1 Samuel 14:47, 48). Noting that David and God shared occupations (1 Samuel 16:11), try to list some heart characteristics God seeks in a leader (Psalm 23).

🎬 What is God calling you to do? How do you know? Paraphrase Jeremiah 1:4-10, making it a personal call from God to you.

IN CONCLUSION

David was one of the greatest figures in biblical history. Yet Samuel was looking for someone big enough to serve and Jesse was thinking of someone old enough to serve. What matters to God, however, is having someone with the heart to serve.

OTHER APPLICATIONS

Use this clip to introduce a sermon, lesson, or devotion on qualifications for service from Matthew 20:20-28 or Luke 22:24-30.

"SCENE" HIM BEFORE?

Veteran actor Nehemiah Persoff (Yentl's father) is probably best known as the voice of Papa Mousekewitz in *An American Tail* (1986) and the following animated features in that series.

THEME

Gideon, overcoming fear

THE FILM

The King and I

Not Rated

Year Released: 1956

Start—3:42 (after overture)

"They look so cruel, Mother."

End—5:55

Anna and Louis walk away from bodyguard whistling nervously

IN THE FACE OF FEAR

Judges 6:11-16

TO BEGIN

Tell about a time when you were deathly afraid. Of what were you afraid? How do you fight such fear? What do you think of this method?

THE CLIP

Mrs. Anna Leonowens (Deborah Kerr) and her son Louis (Rex Thompson) arrive in Bangkok, where she has contracted to educate the children of the royal household.

Arriving in Bangkok, Anna and Louis discuss a way to overcome fear.

FOR DISCUSSION

☞ Of what are Anna and Louis afraid? What do you think are the bases of that fear? Why does Louis want to avoid fear? In the story of Gideon we find that we too have a Father who does not want us to fear.

☞ Where was Gideon and what was he doing as this story opens (Judges 6:11, 12)? Why? Imagine his emotional state. With that in mind, what surprises you about the title with which the angel addresses him? What makes the difference between the angel's assessment of Gideon's strength and Gideon's own assessment? See Ephesians 6:10.

☞ Have you ever said, "I could do great things for God if only . . ."? Compare Judges 6:13, 14 with 2

Corinthians 12:7-10. How might have Gideon and Paul completed that statement? Summarize the answers given by the angel and by God. (Compare the phrases "in the strength you have" and "in weakness.") God shows grace by using people who have not earned that privilege. How does God's grace demonstrate his power?

🎤 Examine a deflated basketball. Of what value is it in that state? Inflate it. How has its value changed? Can you see, touch, smell, or taste the substance that caused this transformation? Read Judges 6:15, 16 and John 3:5-8. Is partnership with God an equal partnership? Explain.

🎤 Using a concordance find verses that contain the phrase "fear not" or an equivalent. Choose seven of these verses, meditating upon one of them each day during quiet times with God this week.

IN CONCLUSION

The secret of overcoming fear is far more than the self-delusion of "whistling a happy tune"! It is embracing the power we have because of God's presence. It is recognizing that God shows his strength by using weak vessels to fulfill his commission. And it is resting in the pledge that God is our partner, fighting with us in frightening circumstances.

OTHER APPLICATIONS

Use this clip to introduce a sermon, lesson, or devotion on overcoming fear from 1 John 4:13-18.

INSIDE INFORMATION

Deborah Kerr's singing voice was dubbed by Marni Nixon. Nixon has been the invisible singing voice of many including Maria in *West Side Story* (1964), Eliza Doolittle in *My Fair Lady* (1964), and most recently as Grandmother Fa in *Mulan* (1997).

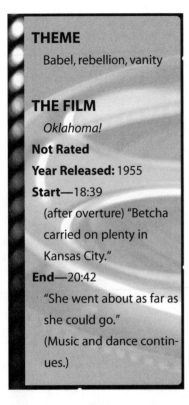

IS PROGRESS GOOD?

Genesis 11:1-9

TO BEGIN

How is life different than it was fifty years ago? How is it better? How is it worse? This character saw some interesting changes in his lifetime.

THE CLIP

Two cowboys win the hearts of their sweethearts in Oklahoma territory at the turn of the twentieth century.

In this scene, Will Parker (Gene Nelson) sings about the modern miracles he witnessed in the big city.

FOR DISCUSSION

⚑ What positive changes did Will see in Kansas City? Was there any "modern" thing there that may not have been good? A famous account in Scripture teaches us that progress is not always good.

⚑ Circle all of the first person pronouns (we, us, ourselves) in Genesis 11:3, 4. How would you say the attitudes of the people of Babel were different from those of the believers of the early church (Acts 4:32-35)? Complete this thought after comparing these two groups of people: "Progress is not good when its only purpose is _____, but it can be good when its purpose is _____."

⚑ Consider the command given to the people of the

world in both Genesis 1:28 and 9:1. Reread Genesis 11:4. From the actions of the people of Shinar, do you believe they intended to obey these earlier commands of God? Complete this thought: "Progress is not good when the intent of the innovator is to _____."

☗ Compare the story of the tower of Babel (especially 11:5-9) with the state of all humankind as described by Paul in Romans 1:18-32 (especially v. 22). Consider what each group (the men of Shinar and the godless and wicked men) tried to accomplish and describe the long-term results of their "progress."

☗ Make a list of ideas that are labeled "progressive" today. Include items such as naturalistic evolution, safe sex, and same-sex marriage. Gather your thoughts and then turn to another member in your group and explain from the lessons of Genesis 11:1-9 why you believe that a particular item on that list is a modern-day tower of Babel.

OTHER APPLICATIONS

Use this clip to introduce a sermon, lesson, or devotion on rebelling against God from Psalm 2.

OOPS!

Although the film is set on the plains of the Oklahoma territory, mountains are clearly visible in the background at the end of this clip. That's because the producers thought Arizona "looked more like Oklahoma" and shot it there instead!

IN CONCLUSION

Progress is not good if its sole purpose is to satisfy our selfish tendencies. Progress is dangerous when we seek to use it to challenge God's sovereignty. Finally, progress can bring long-term damage to us if it is not in accordance to God's will. Just because "everything's up-to-date in Kansas City" (or anywhere else) doesn't mean it is good!

THEME

destruction of God's work, divided kingdom, rebellion of Jeroboam

THE FILM

Camelot

Rated G

Year Released: 1967

Start—2:35:31

(55:00 from beginning of second act; 20:00 from end of movie)

Song "Guenevere" begins.

End—2:42:56

(1:01:34 from beginning of second act)

"Shall I save the timbers for her next stake?"

A KINGDOM DIVIDED

1 Kings 12:1-20

TO BEGIN

Find a picture of the flag of the Confederacy, the "Stars and Bars." What does this flag represent to you? Though it is nearly a century and a half old, does this flag still stir controversy? Give examples and explain. Here is another emotional story of a nation being divided.

THE CLIP

The marriage of King Arthur (Richard Harris) and Guenevere (Vanessa Redgrave) is examined in this musical version of T. H. White's *The Once and Future King.*

Arthur and Mordred (David Hemmings) verbally spar as the results of the affair between Guenevere and Lancelot (Franco Nero) destroy Camelot.

FOR DISCUSSION

☞ What caused the division of Camelot? What was the final result? The nation of Israel also weathered a destructive civil war. Let's try to determine the causes of it.

☞ Complete this sentence: "Someday when I am rich and powerful, I'll _____." Is there any correlation between increase in power and decrease in compassion? Summarize the events of 1 Kings 12:1-15. How is that correlation evident in this case? Read Jesus' words about leadership (Mark 9:33-37). If Jesus had been among Rehoboam's advisors, what would you imagine that he would say?

⛏ In April of 2001, the city of Cincinnati, Ohio, was placed under curfew for a few days because of rioting that occurred in that city. Try to find a news story from the library or Internet on these or other riots of recent memory. What are some of the many causes of sudden outbreaks of violence such as these? Compare these riots to the ones described in 1 Kings 12:16-20. Explain how such events illustrate the truth of Jesus' words in Matthew 5:12-24.

⛏ "Civil religion" is the practice of using religious rituals and allegiance to solidify the political power of a nation. Do you know of any examples in the world today of how religion and patriotism are hopelessly entangled? What are some results? Could the events of 1 Kings 12:25-33 be described as civil religion? Explain. Notice that Jesus' followers desired to mix religion and patriotism (John 6:14, 15). Describe, and attempt to explain Jesus' reaction.

⛏ These same factors can destroy personal relationships. On three blank adhesive labels write, "Control Freak," "Ticking Time Bomb," and "Pious Zealot." If you were to ask members of your family, your company, or your church, would they put one of those labels on you? Which one? Why? Tear it up but keep the pieces with you as a reminder that you wish to extinguish such behaviors in your life.

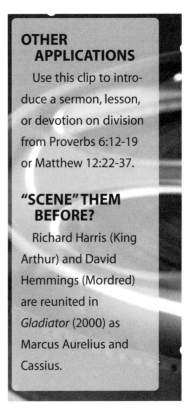

OTHER APPLICATIONS

Use this clip to introduce a sermon, lesson, or devotion on division from Proverbs 6:12-19 or Matthew 12:22-37.

"SCENE" THEM BEFORE?

Richard Harris (King Arthur) and David Hemmings (Mordred) are reunited in *Gladiator* (2000) as Marcus Aurelius and Cassius.

IN CONCLUSION

Like Camelot, Israel endured a painful civil war. Nations are divided when tyranny replaces servanthood, when anger turns to violence, and when patriotism becomes idolatry. So are families, companies, and churches.

MIDNIGHT SONGS
Acts 16:16-34

TO BEGIN

Make two lists. Entitle the first, "I have every reason to be happy because" Entitle the second, "Little things like this just ruin my day." Here is a classic picture of someone who was happy despite his immediate circumstance.

THE CLIP

In 1927, Don Lockwood (Gene Kelly) and Lina Lamont (Jean Hagen) are a famous on-screen romantic pair. When Lockwood meets Kathy Selden (Debbie Reynolds), however, true romance proves to be much greater than the film variety.

In this signature scene, even a rainstorm cannot dampen Lockwood's joy.

FOR DISCUSSION

☞ What reason does Don have to be miserable? What causes him to have joy despite his physical discomfort? The Bible tells a memorable story of others who sang in less than ideal circumstances.

☞ Using a Bible encyclopedia or other reference, gain an understanding of the conditions of a Roman prison, especially what it meant to be beaten with rods, placed in stocks, and placed in the inner cell (Acts 16:22-24). Did the crime of Paul and Silas merit this treatment (vv. 16-21)? What was the true reason for their suffering? How do Peter's words relate to this situation? See 1 Peter 2:20b-25; 3:13, 14; 4:12, 13.

☞ Circle the words, "were listening to them" in Acts 16:25. Substitute the words "heard them." In what way did the meaning change? Compare this verse to Philippians 1:12-14. What is the relationship between joy in suffering and the acceptance of our message?

☞ Later when Paul was challenged to prove that he was an effective minister of the gospel (2 Corinthians 11:16-30), he included this imprisonment in his "credentials" (v. 25). Why might that argument seem strange? Imagine a news interview with the Philippian jailer after the events of Acts 16:25-34. What might he say when asked if he thinks that Paul's behavior in suffering made him an effective apostle?

☞ In the original language, 1 Thessalonians 5:16 is the shortest verse in the New Testament (two letters shorter than John 11:35)! At the end of each day this week, write a one-paragraph commentary on this short verse by applying it to an unpleasant event in your life that day.

THE CONCLUSION

Unjustly arrested, beaten, and confined, Paul and Silas had no apparent reason for joy. Yet they knew their joy came from freeing the oppressed, from giving others the opportunity to hear about God's goodness, and from helping others be changed by God's power. Let's be singing in his reign!

OTHER APPLICATIONS

Use this clip to introduce a sermon, lesson, or devotion about joy in adversity from Philippians 4:4-13 or James 1:2-8.

INSIDE INFORMATION

Gene Kelly *was* singing in adversity. He had a 103-degree fever when this scene was filmed!

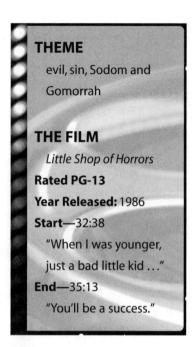

THEME

evil, sin, Sodom and Gomorrah

THE FILM

Little Shop of Horrors

Rated PG-13

Year Released: 1986

Start—32:38

"When I was younger, just a bad little kid ..."

End—35:13

"You'll be a success."

PORTRAITS OF EVIL
Genesis 19:1-29

TO BEGIN

Write the letters E, V, I, L down the side of a piece of paper. Define the word by using words or phrases beginning with each letter. Does the person in this clip fit your definition?

THE CLIP

Seymour Krelborn (Rick Moranis) is a nerdy florist who discovers a carnivorous plant.

In this scene we discover the identity of Audrey's (Ellen Greene) sadistic boyfriend, Orin Scrivello, D.D.S. (Steve Martin).

FOR DISCUSSION

☤ What characteristics do you see in Dr. Scrivello that mark him as being evil? Is evil only aggressive, sadistic actions, or is it more? In the story of Sodom and Gomorrah we see three distinct portraits of evil.

☤ From Genesis 19:1-11; Deuteronomy 32:31-33; and Ezekiel 16:49, 50 describe the morality of a citizen of Sodom. Note the conversation between Lot and the visitors in Genesis 19:1-3, underlining the phrase, "insisted so strongly." What might that indicate about Lot's perception of his neighbors? What do you think motivated and what limited the behavior of the residents of Sodom? To whom would you compare such people in our world today?

☤ Note the conversations taking place in Genesis

19:12-14. Speculate upon the relationship Lot had had with his sons-in-law. What type of moral/ethical/religious guidance would you guess Lot had given in the past? Explain why apathy toward the Lord's message is another face of evil. Paraphrase God's words to Ezekiel (2:3-8), imagining that they were spoken by God to Lot early in his stay in Sodom.

☞ Summarize the story of Lot's wife (Genesis 19:15-17, 23-26). Do you believe her glance was merely curiosity, or was it something else? Paraphrase 1 John 2:15-17 so that it reads as a warning to Lot's wife.

☞ Talk radio personality Dr. Laura Schlessinger refers to culturally accepted practices that hurt the innocent as "everyday evil." She argues that because practices such as no-fault divorce and abortion, for example, are common, we are blind to the immorality of these practices. Look inward. Ask God to show you an everyday evil (vicious temper, selfishness, lust) in your own life and to give you the strength to address it.

IN CONCLUSION

It is easy to characterize evil as outrageous acts of cruelty. Yet evil may have more benign faces. Evil may be marked with obvious, repulsive deeds, but also by apathy, or by loving this world more than loving God.

OTHER APPLICATIONS

Use this clip to introduce a sermon, lesson, or devotion about evil from Leviticus 20; 1 Corinthians 6:9-11; or Galatians 5:19-21.

INSIDE INFORMATION

The members of the film's "Greek Chorus" are all named after '50s/'60s girl singing groups: The Ronettes, The Chiffons, and The Crystals.

A SECOND CHANCE
John 21:1-23

TO BEGIN

What is a "Dear John (Jane)" letter? Have you ever written one? Received one? Tell about it. Here is a "Dear John" letter in song.

THE CLIP

U.S. Navy nurse Nellie Forbush (Mitzi Gaynor) falls in love with French planter Emile de Becque (Rossano Brazzi) while stationed in the Solomon Islands during World War II.

In this well-known scene, Ensign Forbush sings of her intentions to end her relationship with Emile.

FOR DISCUSSION

☞ What does Forbush intend to do? Why? Do you find it easier to sever a relationship rather than work to heal one? The Bible relates an incident that shows how Jesus deals with those who disappoint him.

☞ Compare the events of Luke 5:1-11 to those of John 21:1-14. Knowing that Peter was bitterly disappointed in himself for having denied Jesus (Luke 22:60-62), what is the significance in the similarity of these two fishing trips? What do you think Jesus is saying by recreating this benchmark event of Peter's life?

☞ Read John 13:36-38; 18:15-18, 25-27. Notice the reappearance of the number three in John 21:15-17. Speculate upon the significance of questioning and commissioning Peter three times. What does that say about our ability to sin and Christ's power to forgive and restore (Matthew 18:21, 22)?

🖥 Recall a time when you let your boss down. Were you ever given similar responsibilities again? If so, how much time or what conditions came before your reinstatement? From what you can gather from John 21:18-23, does it appear that Jesus would be giving Peter less challenging or less dangerous assignments as a result of his betrayal? Review the first chapters of the book of Acts, especially 1:15-17; 2:14; 3:11-16; 4:8-12; and 5:15. Does it appear that Peter received a demotion because of his betrayal? Why not? What can you deduce about God's forgiveness?

🖥 Read 1 Peter 2:25. Now paraphrase Peter's words into his confession, recalling the events of John 21. Use the form, "I was _____, but now, _____." Now consider the forgiveness you have received in your life. Rewrite the paraphrase in this same form, recalling how Jesus has forgiven and restored you despite your failures.

IN CONCLUSION

When we disappoint Jesus, he doesn't "wash us out of his hair." Rather, he renews his original call, he demonstrates forgiveness greater than our sin, and he encourages us with even greater challenges and responsibilities.

OTHER APPLICATIONS

Use this clip to introduce a sermon, lesson, or devotion on second chances from Psalm 51 or Acts 9:1-19.

INSIDE INFORMATION

Early casting considerations for the role of Nellie Forbush included Doris Day, Audrey Hepburn, and Elizabeth Taylor.

SIN IN THE CAMP
Joshua 7:1-26

TO BEGIN

Divide into pairs for a three-legged race. With teammates standing side-by-side, tie the inner legs of each pair together. Have teams race two or three at a time. Can a team be successful if one member is not involved in the race? How is that truth illustrated in this clip?

THE CLIP

This lively musical pairs the unlikely combination of gamblers and street missionaries in New York City.

Nicely-Nicely Johnson (Stubby Kaye) sings about how one sin affects the rest of the community.

FOR DISCUSSION

🎥 Explain the meaning of Nicely's song. How did he rock the boat to Heaven? The story of Achan illustrates the impact sin can have.

🎥 Describe the actions taken by Achan (Joshua 6:17-19; 7:1; 20, 21). Why did he do it? How did he think he could get away with it? Imagine that you were Achan's friend and suspected what he was considering. Paraphrase the words of Jesus (Luke 8:16-18) to try to convince Achan to change his mind.

🎥 List some offenses that many label as "victimless crimes." Choose one and argue that such an offense has an effect on more than the person committing it. Why would have Achan considered his offense to be victimless? Explain why he was wrong (Joshua 7:2-13). How does this illustrate the church as the body of Christ (1 Corinthians 12:25-27)? How did robbing or not robbing God of what is his affect the nation of Israel in later years (Malachi 3:9-12)?

Read about the personal consequences that Achan suffered as a result of his sin (Joshua 7:14-26). You are Achan's defense attorney. You argue from God's law that stealing is not a capital offense (Exodus 22:1-15). The prosecutor argues that Achan's sin was not theft, but idolatry (Exodus 20:1-6) because in spite of all that God had done for him, Achan wanted more. He refused to trust God for his needs, and not only stole, but stole that which belonged to God alone. In what ways do we practice this same idolatry today?

Read James 5:16. Do you have a Christian friend to whom you can be held accountable? If so, make some time this week to meet with him or her, discuss your personal struggles, and pray together. If not, pray that God will direct you to such a person.

IN CONCLUSION

Is your sin "no big deal"? Recognize that no sin is ever really secret, that it does affect others around you, and that it will eventually cause you harm. It's time to "sit down, you're rockin' the boat"!

OTHER APPLICATIONS

Use this clip to introduce a sermon, lesson, or devotion on community responsibility from Matthew 5:13-15 or Ephesians 4:7-16.

INSIDE INFORMATION

This movie is based on the stories of Damon Runyon, an American short-story writer and companion to Al Capone, Jack Dempsey, and Babe Ruth. Runyon gained fame with his tales of gambling, racing, and the criminal world.

THEME
golden calf, rebellion, stubbornness

THE FILM
My Fair Lady
Not Rated
Year Released: 1964
Start—9:45
"Woman! Cease this detestable boo-hooing instantly ..."
End—12:45
"Why can't the English learn to speak?"

STUBBORNNESS

Exodus 32:1-35

TO BEGIN

When was the last time you said, "Oops, I did it again"? Do you tend to make the same mistake over and over again? Does that frustrate anyone around you? Notice this man's frustration over repeated errors.

THE CLIP

Snobbish phonetics Professor Henry Higgins (Rex Harrison) wagers that he can take a flower girl (Audrey Hepburn) and make her presentable in high society.

Professor Higgins bemoans the inability of Englishmen to learn the English language.

FOR DISCUSSION

⚞ What repeated errors frustrated Professor Higgins? What do you think causes these kinds of errors? The Bible talks about much more serious errors that people constantly make.

⚞ Recall a time during your school days when your teacher stepped out of the room and did not return for a period of time. Describe the changes that took place in that room as time passed. How is that occurrence similar to what happened when Moses spent an extended time with God on the mountain (Exodus 32:1-4)? How does this story compare to the parable Jesus told about the wicked servant (Matthew 24:45-51)? How do we make this same type of mistake in our lives?

82

🛱 Jot down the first two or three words that come to mind when you hear the word "worship." Look up the word in the dictionary and discover its derivation. Do you often find yourself paying more attention to the mechanics of worship rather than the attitudes necessary for true "worth-ship"? Do you think that was the problem with the Israelites (Exodus 32:5-8)? Explain. When we ask, "What is the right way to worship," what is God's answer? See Micah 6:6-8.

🛱 Have you ever been caught red-handed? When confronted, did you admit your mistake, or did you make an excuse? Notice Aaron's response when confronted by Moses (Exodus 32:22-24). On a scale of one to ten, how would you rate the quality of his excuse? Defend your rating. What are some of the excuses people make today for refusing to give God the respect he deserves? Use the words of Romans 1:18-20 to refute one or more of these excuses.

🛱 Imagine the Israelites asking these questions of God in this story: "Are you really there?" "Aren't you impressed?" "Don't you believe me?" Try to catch yourself asking any of those questions of God in the coming week.

IN CONCLUSION

In the golden calf incident we see mistakes that God's people make repeatedly throughout history. Why can't we learn that God is still working even when we do not see immediate activity? Why can't we learn that worship is a matter of lifestyle rather than ritual? Why can't we learn that our excuses for our disobedience are hollow and meaningless?

OTHER APPLICATIONS

Use this clip to introduce a sermon, lesson, or devotion on stubbornness from 1 Corinthians 10:1-13; Galatians 3:1-5; or James 4:1-12.

INSIDE INFORMATION

This musical is an adaptation of the play *Pygmalion* by George Bernard Shaw.

THEME
blessings and hardships, justice of God

THE FILM
Jailhouse Rock
Not Rated
Year Released: 1957
Start—51:10
"OK, we're ready."
End—53:20
Song ends.

WHY LOVE GOD?
Job 1:1-22

TO BEGIN

Make a thank-you card for your mother. On the front of it write: "I don't know how you could still love me after I . . ." Aren't you glad your mom's love didn't come with the same conditions described in this song?

THE CLIP

After serving time in prison, young Vince Everett (Elvis Presley) becomes a rock star.

Peggy Van Alden (Judy Tyler) watches as Vince records his first single.

FOR DISCUSSION

☞ Summarize the conditions put on relationships in this song. Do you know anyone who lives by such a philosophy? What are the results? The story of Job explores how one can have a relationship with God in a world that doesn't always "Treat Me Nice."

☞ Compare Job 1:8 and John 15:14. How do Job's actions match Jesus' criteria for friendship with him? List the actions that Job took that indicated his love for God (Job 1:1-5).

☞ A pop song of several years ago asked, "What's Love Got to Do With It?" The singer argued that love is a "sweet old-fashioned notion" and is nothing more that a name given to baser impulses. If you can find the song, play it and compare it to Satan's description of Job's love for God (Job 1:9, 10). What did Satan claim was Job's motivation for behaving as he did? What happens when that is one's sole motivation for obeying God (Luke 8:13, 14)?

🎬 Read Job 1:11-22. How did Satan attempt to prove his argument? How successful was he in doing so? Give Job a report card for loving God. Along with a letter grade, explain the reason for your grade in a sentence or two. From Job 1:22; James 1:13; and 1 Peter 5:6-9, make a list of dos and don'ts for facing unexpected hardships.

🎬 Part of Job's strategy for being true to God despite hardship was summarized when he said, "Shall we accept good from God and not trouble?" (Job 2:10). Consciously work to develop this philosophy with a prayer journal this week. For every request for help in difficulty that you record, try to record two prayers of thanksgiving for blessings you enjoy. Have you noticed how we are more likely to say, "Why me?" when faced with hardship rather than blessings? Try to reverse that tendency in yourself.

IN CONCLUSION

God was pleased that Job made a conscious choice to love him. Satan set out to prove that Job's obedience was a response to intimidation and bribery. Job, however, remained faithful even without understanding his circumstances.

OTHER APPLICATIONS

Use this clip to introduce a sermon, lesson, or devotion on the justice of God from James 5:7-16.

INSIDE INFORMATION

Elvis refused to watch this movie because of Judy Tyler's tragic death in an automobile accident just before it was released.

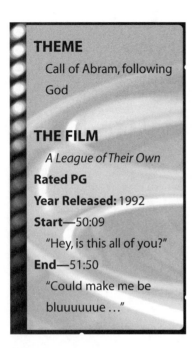

CALLED BY GOD
Genesis 12:1-5

TO BEGIN

Quickly improvise the following skit: A telemarketer interrupts a family at dinner. What does the caller want? How likely is it that the call will receive a positive response? Watch this clip of another rather unattractive appeal.

THE CLIP

During World War II a women's professional baseball league is formed.

In this scene the team makes an unauthorized stop at a honky-tonk. Unattractive Marla Hooch (Megan Cavanagh) sings a torch song to a man in the bar.

FOR DISCUSSION

☙ Describe Marla's plea in this song. How is it presented? How is it motivated? Why does it seem unlikely that someone would respond positively to such a call? Yet the Bible tells about an even more outrageous call from God to Abram.

☙ Responding to God's call was costly for Abram. After reviewing Genesis 12:1 and Hebrews 11:8, 9, list inconveniences, dangers, and lifestyle changes that Abram would have faced when responding to God's call. Compare Abram's situation with that of the twelve apostles in Matthew 10. How does understanding Abram's call help us understand what Jesus was saying in Matthew 10:34-39?

⌦ God's promises often sound totally unbelievable at first. Compare God's promises to Abram (Genesis 12:2, 3) to his promises to Peter (Matthew 16:15-19). From what you know about these two men at the time of these promises, explain why it would be ridiculous to believe that those promises could be fulfilled by their efforts alone.

⌦ Although God called Abram, who else was affected by that call? (See Genesis 12:4, 5.) How is this similar to the responses of Cornelius (Acts 10:24), Lydia (Acts 16:14, 15), and the Philippian jailer (Acts 16:29-34)?

⌦ What would God say to you if he were to call you right now, as he called Abram? On a sheet of paper list *inconveniences, dangers,* and *lifestyle changes* God would want you to make to follow him more fully. Then list the *rewards* God may want to give you when you follow. Then list the *names of others* that would be affected when you answer that call. Use these lists as a prayer guide this next week.

IN CONCLUSION

The call of God to us is just as outrageous as his call to Abram. He wants his children to leave their comfort zones, to trust him for rewards that they are powerless to attain on their own, and to share that call with those closest to them. Listen for God's call, because "it had to be you!"

OTHER APPLICATIONS

Use this clip to introduce a sermon, lesson, or devotion on being called by God from Judges 6:11-16; Isaiah 6; or Acts 26.

INSIDE INFORMATION

This film is based upon the All-American Girls Professional Baseball League that was in existence between 1943-1954. The behavior in this scene was expressly prohibited by rule three of the league agreement: "Smoking or drinking is not permissible in public places. Liquor drinking will not be permissible under any circumstances. Other intoxicating drinks in limited portions with after-game meal only, will be allowed." The penalty for the first offense was five dollars. A ten-dollar penalty would be paid for a second offense, with suspension being the penalty for a third.

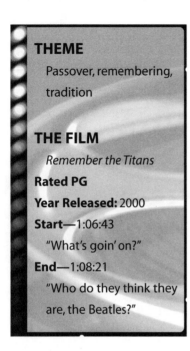

THEME

Passover, remembering, tradition

THE FILM

Remember the Titans

Rated PG

Year Released: 2000

Start—1:06:43

"What's goin' on?"

End—1:08:21

"Who do they think they are, the Beatles?"

CEREMONY

Exodus 12:1-28

TO BEGIN

For what do you want to be known? What do you consider your personal trademark? Ask others in the room to tell you the first thing that comes into their minds when they think of you. Here is a football team who developed a ceremony that communicated who they were.

THE CLIP

Herman Boone (Denzel Washington) is hired as the football coach of a newly racially-integrated high school in Alexandria, in the early 1970s.

In this clip the team demonstrates its unity with an unusual warm-up drill that would become its unique signature.

FOR DISCUSSION

Describe the Titan's warm-up ceremony. What do you think it was meant to communicate? Do you think it was effective? In the book of Exodus, God gave his nation a ceremony that became its signature.

Summarize the ceremony of the Passover (Exodus 12:1-10). Explain the significance of the lamb, blood, and bread without yeast (unleavened), using a Bible dictionary if necessary. What does the calendar change (v. 2) say about the importance of this ceremony? If the power of God to deliver his people is of primary importance in the Old Testament, what is of similar importance in the New Testament (1 Corinthians 15:3, 4; 5:6-8)?

☞ The Passover ceremony was not only significant for *what* was done, but also for *how* it was done. How is the urgency of this festival's message illustrated (Exodus 12:11-13)? Is there anything equally urgent for us as Christians (2 Corinthians 6:1, 2; Hebrews 3:12-15)? Explain.

☞ Read Exodus 12:24-28, circling the phrase, "lasting ordinance." Why is that phrase so important? How were the people to guarantee that Passover be a lasting ordinance? Explain the ceremony that is the New Testament Passover (1 Corinthians 11:23-26). Is it also to be a lasting ordinance? Explain.

☞ Passover summarized what it meant to be God's nation. In a paragraph or two, explain why the Lord's Supper symbolizes what it means to be a Christian. Keep that in mind when you next keep this ordinance.

IN CONCLUSION

The Passover was a ceremony that summarized what it meant to be Jewish. Therefore, the celebration of God's redemption of his nation from Egypt was given the highest priority in worship, was a matter of urgency, and was a lasting memorial. As believers we see all of these elements in our signature ceremony, the Lord's Supper.

OTHER APPLICATIONS

Use this clip to introduce a sermon, lesson, or devotion on the Passover from Deuteronomy 16:1-8 or Psalm 81.

OOPS!

Set in 1971, most players wear helmet face masks not available until the early 1980s.

THEME
Character, Joseph in Egypt

THE FILM
Young Frankenstein
Rated PG
Year Released: 1974
Start—1:16:25
Outside the theater.
End—1:22:10
"It's nothing, nothing I tell you!"

CHARACTER

Genesis 39:1-23

TO BEGIN

Explain the saying, "You can take the boy out of the country, but you can't take the country out of the boy." How might it apply to this clip?

THE CLIP

Dr. Frederick Frankenstein (Gene Wilder) finds it difficult to distance himself from the reputation of his monster-creating grandfather.

In this scene, Frederick demonstrates the capabilities of his creature (Peter Boyle) to a scientific gathering.

FOR DISCUSSION

☙ At what point did you laugh the hardest at this clip? What was the basis for the humor? Explain how the costume of the monster differed from his true character. Joseph, son of Jacob, also had character that transcended any costume he wore or role he played.

☙ What is a "rags to riches" story? Can you think of any such true stories from history? Does Genesis 39:1-6a tell such a story? Describe as many distinct steps in Joseph's rise in status as you can. Explain the significance of the phrase, "the Lord was with Joseph," to Joseph's success. What were some ways that God's presence might have been noticed in Joseph's character? See Philippians 2:12-16.

☙ Genesis 39:6b-20a tells the story of how God's

person, though in a role of subservience, refused to compromise morally. In what ways is this story similar to one told in Daniel 3? In what ways does it differ? Consider the statement: "In the business world, it is sometimes wise for a Christian to leave his convictions outside the office door." Reread Daniel 3:16-18 and formulate a response to it.

🎥 Imagine interviewing the wife of Potiphar a few days after Joseph's arrest. If she were asked to speculate upon Joseph's conditions and circumstances at that time, what might she have said? Compare those thoughts to the true story found in Genesis 39:20b-23. Refer to this story and James 5:3, 4 to explain the difference.

🎥 Joseph had no choice but to wear the garments of slavery, dependence, and persecution. What "garments" do you wear that are outside of your control (socioeconomic status, personal tragedy, disability, etc.)? Meditate upon Matthew 5:1-12 this week, asking God to allow your character to be strong enough to endure any such circumstances.

IN CONCLUSION

Joseph's true character stood out regardless of his situation. Social standing could not hide his competence. Dependence could not compromise his morality. Persecution could not steal his success. No matter how the world "dressed up" Joseph, his true character showed through!

OTHER APPLICATIONS

Use this clip to introduce a sermon, lesson, or devotion on displaying good character from Ephesians 4:20-24 or James 3:13-18.

INSIDE INFORMATION

Before deciding to pursue a career in acting, Peter Boyle was a monk in Christian Brothers order.

THEME
compromise, the devil, Satan

THE FILM
Ferris Bueller's Day Off
Rated PG-13
Year Released: 1986
Start—1:00:38
Overhead view of parade.
End—1:05:15
Ferris waves to the crowd.

DON'T LET THE DEVIL IN
Ephesians 4:25-28

TO BEGIN
Have you ever felt that someone was trying to take over your life? Perhaps you let your guard down somewhat and before you knew it, someone else was taking over! Maybe it looked a lot like this.

THE CLIP
Bored with high school, Ferris Bueller (Matthew Broderick) and his friends Sloane (Mia Sara) and Cameron (Alan Ruck) play hooky and take to the streets of Chicago.

In this scene, Ferris disappears only to reappear as the star of an Oktoberfest float.

FOR DISCUSSION
☞ Cameron says that Ferris is going to be "a fry cook on Venus." What do you think he meant by that? How does Ferris demonstrate his ability to survive and thrive in unlikely places in this scene? Although this character seems endearing, why would you be concerned about a Ferris Bueller in real life? The Bible tells of one who wants to take over our lives (Ephesians 4:27) and outlines a strategy for combating that enemy.

☞ "Oh, what a tangled web we weave, When first we practice to deceive!"(Sir Walter Scott, "Marmion.") Can you think of a time in your life when a simple lie started a chain reaction of problems? By comparing Ephesians 4:25; John 8:44; and John 14:6, construct a hypothesis that explains why Scott's famous quotation is true. Why does compromising truth give Satan a foothold?

🎥 What significance do the words of Ephesians 4:25b have to v. 26? By comparing these verses with Matthew 5:21-24; 6:12, explain how we give the devil a foothold when we let anger destroy relationships with our Christian brothers and sisters.

🎥 If you were to give a completely honest answer to the question, "Why do you have a job?" what would your answer be? What better answer is found in Ephesians 4:28? Read Luke 22:24-32 carefully. How do we use wealth, position, and power to subjugate others and elevate ourselves? How does that self-centered lifestyle give the devil a foothold?

🎥 On each of three note cards, write one of the following words: dishonesty, anger, arrogance. As you look at each one, ask the Lord to bring to mind a situation in which you have allowed each trait to separate you from God and his people. Continue this exercise daily this week, praying for direction in correcting each situation.

IN CONCLUSION

Don't let the devil hijack your parade! Live a life marked with truth, forgiveness, and self-sacrifice.

OTHER APPLICATIONS

Use this clip to introduce a sermon, lesson, or devotion about overcoming Satan from Matthew 16:21-23; James 4:7; or 1 Peter 5:8, 9.

OOPS!

Ferris is supposed to be skipping school, but the crowd at the parade is filled with school-aged children.

THEME

God's way, Ten
Commandments

THE FILM

Big

Rated PG

Year Released: 1988

Start—37:58

Josh steps on keyboard.

End—40:07

"Just saved me a trip to
the gym, son."

INSTRUCTION

Exodus 20:1-21

TO BEGIN

What relatively meaningless lesson or skill did you
learn in childhood that you have never forgotten?
Would these tunes be among your unforgotten
lessons?

THE CLIP

Twelve-year-old Josh Baskin (Tom Hanks) makes a
wish to be "big" and finds himself in an adult body
literally overnight.

During a trip to the toy store, Josh meets his boss
(Robert Loggia) and joins him in this memorable
instrumental duet.

FOR DISCUSSION

☞ Have you ever played these same tunes on a keyboard? Could you still play them? What makes
certain lessons hard to forget? At Mount Sinai
God gave a basic lesson in morality that has
endured for generations.

☞ List the ways you would show a spouse that you
love him or her. After making this list, label each
item in one or more of the following ways: Place a
"D" by each that demonstrate that you are
devoted to your spouse, forsaking all others. Place
a "S" by each that relates to what you say about
your spouse. Finally, place a "T" by each item on
your list that has to do with spending time with
your beloved. Read Exodus 20:1-8. Consider our
love relationship with God. Mark these verses

with the same code used above. What is the first requirement of a moral life (Matthew 22:37, 38)? Explain how that love is demonstrated by para-phrasing the first four Commandments into a single sentence.

OTHER
APPLICATIONS
Use this clip to intro-duce a sermon, lesson, or devotion on the Ten Commandments from Deuteronomy 5:1-21.

🎬 Read Exodus 20:12, 13 and Genesis 9:6, 7. What do they say about the sanctity of the family and of human life? How are both respect for family and respect for human life absolutely essential for a stable society? What happens when either is com-promised?

**INSIDE
INFORMATION**
This scene was filmed in the ultimate toy store, FAO Schwartz of New York City.

🎬 Imagine that you had the power to become invisi-ble, that you could do whatever you wanted with-out fear of being detected. Acting on your worst impulses, what might you do? How many of your actions would violate the commands of Exodus 20:14-17? In light of the Bible's description of human nature (Jeremiah 17:9), why are these last four Commandments necessary?

🎬 Have you ever tried to be good without God? During a quiet time each day this week, compare the divine moral nature (Exodus 20:3-17) with the carnal moral nature (Romans 1:28-32). Ask God to reveal to you the behaviors and attitudes in you that need to be changed. Ask for his help in becoming more like him.

IN CONCLUSION

The Ten Commandments provide the ultimate framework for moral behavior. God desires that we put him first in our worship, speech, and schedules. He commands us to respect human life by honoring those who granted it to us and by protecting the innocent. Finally, he wants us to have wholesome relationships with others by restraining our desires. These "music lessons" keep us in harmony with our creator.

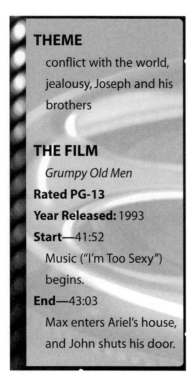

JEALOUSY

Genesis 37:1-11

TO BEGIN

Are you a competitive person? What are some positive results of being in competition? What are some negative results? Here is a clip of two men who have been in competition with one another all their lives.

THE CLIP

John Gustafson (Jack Lemmon) and Max Goldman (Walter Matthau) are two neighbors carrying on a fifty-year feud.

In this scene, both men prepare to call on their new neighbor Ariel (Ann-Margaret).

FOR DISCUSSION

☞ Note the look on John's face at the end of this scene. Though there is no dialogue in this clip, what emotions do you see expressed? Sometimes competition can cause jealousy and anger, even among close friends and family. The Bible tells of a sibling rivalry that evolved into conflict and hatred.

☞ Note the first source of conflict between Jacob's sons (Genesis 37:2). While we may react negatively to a tattletale, why can we assume that Joseph's actions were appropriate? For what reasons can we believe that Joseph's brothers were the guilty parties? Compare Joseph and his brothers to Abel and Cain and then to believers and unbelievers (1 John 3:12, 13).

☞ What item of clothing caused additional conflict among Jacob's sons (Genesis 37:3)? The word describing his robe (*passim* in Hebrew) is used to describe a robe only one other time in Scripture (2 Samuel 13:18). Does the status signified by Tamar's robe help explain why such a robe angered Joseph's brothers? How are those who live faithfully for Jesus similarly dressed (Revelation 7:13-17)? Are the reactions of Joseph's brothers similarly motivated to the reaction of the world to believers (John 15:18, 19; 1 Peter 4:12-16)? In what way?

☞ Has anyone ever told you that he or she wished Christians would keep the Bible and religious views to themselves? Tell about it. Do you think Joseph's brothers felt the same way (Genesis 37:5-11)? Notice a similar dynamic between hatred of the world and those who receive God's Word (John 17:14). Respond to the following question after reading the words of Proverbs 29:18 in a few different translations: "If sharing a vision from God is so controversial, why do it at all?"

☞ Write the words of Romans 12:18 on a note card to carry with you and memorize this week. As you recite the verse, ask God to help you distinguish between avoidable and unavoidable conflicts.

IN CONCLUSION

The jealousy between Joseph and his brothers is not unlike the conflict we have with the world when we try to live as people of faith. Others may feel condemned by our value system, estranged because of our relationship with God, and excluded by our vision of the world. Though we should always work to avoid conflict, we must not be surprised when it exists.

OTHER APPLICATIONS

Use this clip to introduce a sermon, lesson, or devotion on conflict in the world from Matthew 10:17-42.

OOPS!

Not one character in this movie speaks with the accent of someone from a small town in Minnesota where the film claims to be set. Is that important? Ya, yew betcha!

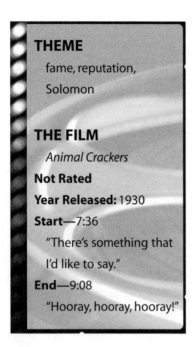

THEME
fame, reputation,
Solomon

THE FILM
Animal Crackers
Not Rated
Year Released: 1930
Start—7:36
"There's something that
I'd like to say."
End—9:08
"Hooray, hooray, hooray!"

A KING'S REPUTATION
1 Kings 10:1-13

TO BEGIN

Imagine that you have the opportunity to host a famous person in your home. What would the encounter be like? What expectations would you have? Watch as this clip introduces an explorer of great reputation.

THE CLIP

Noted explorer, Captain Spaulding (Groucho Marx), returns from Africa and attends a gala party held by Mrs. Rittenhouse (Margaret Dumont). Spaulding is introduced in song.

FOR DISCUSSION

☞ What were some elements of Captain Spaulding's reputation? Did his reputation accurately reflect his character? Give examples. The Bible tells us of a king whose reputation was certainly warranted.

☞ Watch a televised news interview with a political figure. How can you tell whether or not the interviewer is sympathetic to the politics of the interviewee? Were the interview questions hardballs or softballs? Explain and give examples. Read 1 Kings 10:1-3. Speculate upon the Queen of Sheba's attitude toward Solomon as she entered Jerusalem. What kind of interviewer do you think she was? Do you think that the residents of Berea had a similar hardball attitude (Acts 17:10-12)? What does God think of seekers who ask hard questions?

☙ Summarize the queen's observations and her con-
clusions (1 Kings 10:4-9). Did the accomplish-
ments of Solomon achieve the effect God desired
of them (Matthew 5:16; 1 Peter 2:12)?

☙ Contrast the initial approach and the results of the
Queen of Sheba's visit with Solomon (1 Kings
10:10, 13) to the initial approach and results of
the visit of the rich young ruler with Jesus
(Matthew 19:16-22). Imagine that the queen and
the young ruler switched places in history. Retell
both stories with this new cast of characters. Why
were the results so different?

☙ List characteristics of God that drew you to him.
List at least ten items. Now think of a non-
Christian that you know well. If you were to make
the assumption that all of this person's knowledge
of God's character comes from observing your
character, how many items on your list would be
on his or her list? What can you do to improve
your score?

OTHER APPLICATIONS

Use this clip to intro-
duce a sermon, lesson,
or devotion on reputa-
tion from Proverbs 22:1-
6 or Philippians 2:1-18.

INSIDE INFORMATION

"Hooray for Captain
Spaulding" became
Groucho's theme song,
and was featured on his
TV game show, "You Bet
Your Life."

IN CONCLUSION

The story of Solomon and the Queen of Sheba
demonstrates why believers must maintain characters that match their reputations. Honest seekers will
test our reputations to see if we are all we claim to
be. Satisfied seekers will recognize that our goodness is merely a reflection of God's goodness.
Reverent seekers will leave our presence enriched,
having had their own needs met.

THEME

healing, humility, Naaman

THE FILM

Casablanca

Not Rated

Year Released: 1942

Start—36:06

The scene opens with Rick drinking alone.

End—38:42

Focus goes soft on Rick's face and scene ends.

LISTENING TO THE PEONS
2 Kings 5:1-14

TO BEGIN

Tell the famous children's story, "The Emperor's New Clothes." Who is the only character in the story who speaks the truth? Why would a king not have sought advice from him? Who is giving advice in this scene?

THE CLIP

Cynical nightclub owner Rick Blaine (Humphrey Bogart) is reunited with his lost love Ilsa (Ingrid Bergman) in war-torn Africa.

In this famous scene, Sam (Dooley Wilson) tries to advise a forlorn Rick.

FOR DISCUSSION

☞ How does Rick treat Sam's suggestions? Why might that be? Have you ever had your input summarily dismissed by an employer? The story of Naaman demonstrates that great wisdom can come from the mouth of an underling.

☞ Describe Naaman's position and reputation (2 Kings 5:1). Consider the individuals mentioned in the next two verses (vv. 2, 3): Naaman's wife, her foreign servant girl, and a prophet in a foreign land. Using the content from all three of those people, describe the advice Naaman was given. Why would listening to such advice seem illogical for a man in Naaman's position? Paraphrase Proverbs 3:5, 6 to complete this sentence: "Naaman was challenged to . . ."

☛ Consider this parable: The vice president of a major auto manufacturer was having car trouble. He had heard that help was available to him in a dealership in a small town miles away. The president of his company encouraged him to seek that help and called the manager of the dealership. The manager panicked, not knowing how to solve the problem. Then his chief mechanic assured him that he could handle the situation. When the vice president appeared at the dealership, he was given instructions on how he should make the repair from the mechanic's assistant. The vice president was furious.

☛ Note the parallels in this story to 2 Kings 5:4-12. Why do you think Naaman was angry? Similarly, Jesus instructed everyone from peasant to priest with simple stories. How might an attitude similar to Naaman's have kept them from understanding his message (Matthew 13:10-15)?

☛ Compare the conclusion of this story (2 Kings 5:13, 14) to James 4:6-10 and 1 Peter 5:5-7. Summarize the principles you find.

☛ Spend one Sunday observing in a children's Sunday school class, youth meeting, or junior worship. Be ready to learn from little ones.

IN CONCLUSION

Although he was a "great man" and "highly regarded," Naaman learned important lessons from listening to servants when he was hurting. His wife's servant taught him to seek God's messenger, Elisha's servant instructed him to follow simple directions, and his own servant helped him divest himself of his pride. While it may seem romantic in Casablanca for this scene to end with Rick wallowing in despair, why do it when you don't have to?

OTHER APPLICATIONS

Use this clip to introduce a sermon, lesson, or devotion on humility from 1 Corinthians 1:26-31.

OOPS!

The most famous line from Casablanca does not appear in the film at all! Because Sam played "As Time Goes By" earlier in the film for Ilsa, Rick is asking him to play the song again in this scene. But he never uses the well-known line, "Play it again, Sam."

THEME
God's Word, revival

THE FILM
Sister Act
Rated PG
Year Released: 1992
Start—53:38
"Welcome this Sunday morning oh, you few but faithful."
End—58:29
"Come in!"
(For more discussion fodder, continue tape until Bishop O'Hara leaves the office.)

REVIVAL

2 Kings 22

TO BEGIN

Complete this thought: "More people would come to church if . . ." Could you imagine the events of this clip occurring?

THE CLIP

Lounge singer Deloris Van Cartier (Whoopi Goldberg) prepares to testify against the mob. Posing as Sister Mary Clarence, Deloris hides in a convent. The situation brings profound change to both her and the church.

In this scene, Sister Mary Clarence leads her choir in its debut.

FOR DISCUSSION

🎬 What was the reaction of the people in the streets to the change in music? How does their reaction support Mary Clarence's argument with Mother Superior? What do you think Mary Clarence's idea of religious revival might be? Do you agree or disagree with her? A religious revival in the days of King Josiah gives us a biblical view of this topic.

🎬 Edit the accounts found in 2 Kings 22:1-7 and 2 Chronicles 34:1-13 into one story. Can you find any characteristics of Josiah that you believe were responsible for the beginning of religious revival? Summarize them. How many of them do you find in God's words to Solomon three centuries earlier (2 Chronicles 7:14)?

☞ Describe the unexpected discovery made when the temple was repaired (2 Kings 22:8-13; 2 Chronicles 34:14-21). How did Josiah react to this discovery? Imagine that Deuteronomy 17:14-20 was part of the Scripture that Josiah heard. Why might those words in particular have affected Josiah in the way described?

☞ Contrast Josiah's reception of God's Word (2 Kings 23:1-3; 2 Chronicles 34:29-32) to the reception given it by his son Jehoiakim barely twenty years later (Jeremiah 36:1-24). Explain how the words of Paul (1 Thessalonians 5:19-21) apply in each case. Describe how the flames of revival should be fed according to Paul.

☞ Review the roles of Josiah, Hilkiah, and the elders of Judah in this revival. How do each of these correspond to people or positions in your particular congregation? Which role(s) is/are most needed in your congregation now? Explain. Into which role(s) do you fit? What could you be doing to better fulfill your responsibilities?

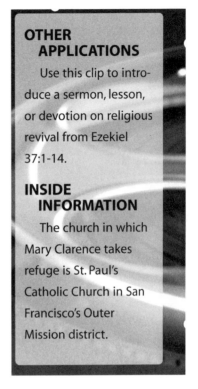

OTHER APPLICATIONS
Use this clip to introduce a sermon, lesson, or devotion on religious revival from Ezekiel 37:1-14.

INSIDE INFORMATION
The church in which Mary Clarence takes refuge is St. Paul's Catholic Church in San Francisco's Outer Mission district.

IN CONCLUSION

Revival is more than getting "butts in the seats." Superficial changes that simply increase church attendance are not enough. Revival begins with a leader who seeks God, continues with a rediscovery of the Word of God, and reaches a climax when the community as a whole repents.

THEME

evangelism, unlikely ministers, woman at the well

THE FILM

The Fighting Kentuckian

Not Rated

Year Released: 1949

Start—54:15

"Uh-uh. Fiddlin' gentlemen through the side door, please."

End—56:50

Laughter and applause.

AN UNLIKELY MINISTER
John 4:1-42

TO BEGIN

Recall or create a simile (a comparison using "like" or "as") to describe someone who is out of place. (For example, "like a fish out of water" or "as conspicuous as my grandmother at a Marilyn Manson concert.") Does another come to mind while you watch this clip?

THE CLIP

In Alabama in 1818, Kentucky militiaman John Breen (John Wayne) falls in love with a French exile and discovers a plot to steal the land her fellow exiles plan to settle on.

Breen finds himself as a featured musician in a string ensemble.

FOR DISCUSSION

☞ Complete this simile: "As out of place as John Wayne in a . . ." How do you think Breen felt in this scene? Have you ever had similar feelings? The Bible tells us that sometimes God calls unlikely recruits.

☞ Who would you guess was the first evangelist for Christ in the New Testament? To see if you were right, read John 4:1-42. What about her social status makes it surprising that she was called for that purpose (vv. 9, 27)? Read 1 Corinthians 1:26-31. What perceived social deficiencies were found in others called to evangelize? Summarize Paul's explanation for God doing this. How do Paul's words also relate to the Samaritan woman?

🔊 Find another, more serious deficiency in this evangelist (John 4:16-18). Imagine that you have a Christian friend who says, "My background is too sinful for the Lord to significantly use me." Reply to him or her using this passage, 1 Corinthians 6:9-11, and 1 Timothy 1:12-14.

🔊 Look at Jesus' commands to his disciples in John 4:35. Assuming that people in that region wore simple, uncolored garments for daily use, could Jesus' command be taken literally? If so, what might have his disciples seen (vv. 28-30)? Describe the surprising degree of success this first evangelist had (vv. 39-42).

🔊 Make a list of ten kingdom tasks that you think it is unlikely Jesus would call you to perform. When you pray this week, ask God, "Am I disqualifying myself for something on this list you would have me do?"

THE CONCLUSION

The first evangelist of the New Testament was an unlikely minister, indeed. Jesus called someone from an unlikely social position, someone from an unseemly moral background, and yet gave her unprecedented success. Let us follow the example of the Samaritan woman. When we are called into God's orchestra, let the music begin!

OTHER APPLICATIONS

Use this clip to introduce a sermon, lesson, or devotion about unlikely ministers from Numbers 22:21-35 or Amos 7:10-17.

"SCENE" HIM BEFORE?

Yes, comic star Oliver Hardy stars with John Wayne as his sidekick, Willie Paine. "That's another fine mess you've gotten us into!"

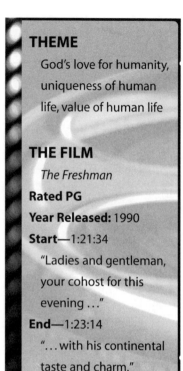

VALUE OF HUMAN LIFE
Genesis 1:26-29

TO BEGIN

What comes to mind when you hear the phrase "one of a kind"? What is the relationship of that phrase to value? What in this clip has great value caused by rarity?

THE CLIP

Clark Kellogg (Matthew Broderick), a freshman in a New York City film school, meets Carmine "Jimmy the Toucan" Sabatini (Marlon Brando), an "importer" bearing a startling resemblance to a cinematic godfather.

In this scene, guests of the underground Gourmet Club meet their main course for the evening, an endangered reptile.

FOR DISCUSSION

☞ Analyze the humor of this clip. Although the Komodo dragon is valuable because of its rarity, why does the use of this song seem out of place? Rarity gives something value, but what other attributes bestow value? In the book of Genesis, the Bible tells us about God's creation of human beings. In these verses we learn three reasons why human life, though not rare nor always beautiful, has infinite value.

☞ Do you have an item or two that is autographed? Describe it (them). What effect does such an autograph have upon the value of an item? What might an autograph signify? See Genesis 1:26, 27;

9:6; Ecclesiastes 7:29; 1 Corinthians 15:45-49; and James 3:9. From what you see there, explain this statement: "Humans are valuable because they are autographed life forms."

🖳 Make a list of appliances in your house. Place a check mark by any item that you would have to replace immediately if it did not function. Although some items on your list may be more costly, would you say they are more valuable? How does humankind's unique function give us value (Genesis 1:28; 9:2; Matthew 28:18-20; Ephesians 2:10)?

🖳 Do you like to be pampered? In what way(s)? How does this type of provision make you feel about your value in the eyes of another? Compare Genesis 1:29; 9:3; and Psalm 37:3, 4. Explain why these verses evidence the value God places upon human life.

🖳 Fill in the blank with the name of a person you know personally: "The world would be better off without _____." Reviewing this lesson, do you think God agrees? This week ask God what you need to do to align your thinking in this matter with his.

THE CONCLUSION

Regardless of the confusion that exists in the world today about the value of human life, the Bible is clear. Man alone is created in God's image. Man alone has been made caretaker of the things of God. Man alone is provided for completely by God.

OTHER APPLICATIONS

Use this clip to introduce a sermon, lesson, or devotion about the value of human life from Psalm 8.

"SCENE" HIM BEFORE?

Burt Parks was a longtime host of the "Miss America Pageant." The theme song that greeted winners for many years is parodied here.

OOPS!

In reality, the population of Komodo dragons in the world is stable. The lizard is neither endangered nor threatened with extinction by humans. This misrepresentation does make for a fun movie though!

Topical Index

Scripture Index